P9-DYZ-182

TAPPING THE
POTENTIAL
OF PARENTS

Patricia A. Edwards

A Strategic Guide to Boosting Student Achievement
Through Family Involvement

Fitchburg Public Library
5530 Lacy Road
Fitchburg, WI 53711

SCHOLASTIC

NEW YORK • TORONTO • LONDON • AUCKLAND • SYDNEY
MEXICO CITY • NEW DELHI • HONG KONG • BUENOS AIRES

Dedication

This book is dedicated in loving memory to my father, John Edwards, and mother, Annie Kate Edwards, for their guidance and love, for stressing the importance of building home-school-community partnerships, and for developing in me the need to care about other people. I wish they had lived to see this book. They would have been extremely proud of me as always.

Scholastic grants teachers permission to photocopy the reproducible pages from this book for classroom use. No other part of this publication may be reproduced in whole or in part, or stored in a retrieval system, or transmitted in any form or by any means, electronic, mechanical, photocopying, recording, or otherwise, without permission of the publisher. For information regarding permission, write to Scholastic Inc., 557 Broadway, New York, NY 10012.

Acquisition Editor: Lois Bridges
Development/Production Editor: Danny Miller
Cover design by Brian LaRossa
Cover photographs: Getty Images, Arabian Eye, Gallo Images, Anthony Strack, The Image Bank
Interior design by Sarah Morrow

ISBN-13: 978-0-545-07477-3
ISBN-10: 0-545-07477-0
Copyright © 2009 by Patricia A. Edwards
All rights reserved. Published by Scholastic Inc.
Printed in the U.S.A.

1 2 3 4 5 6 7 8 9 10   23   15 14 13 12 11 10 09

Contents

Acknowledgments

I want to express my appreciation to the families and teachers who participated in the Home Literacy Project, which I developed to create a structure for families interested in becoming involved in a professional development school in Lansing, Michigan. I would like to thank all of the state and local reading associations, school districts, educational organizations, and colleges and universities for allowing me to share my ideas about how to bridge connections among the home, school, and community.

I would like to thank Tawana Miller (Director of Title 1, Fulton County Schools) and two of her parent liaisons for sharing their ideas on how to communicate with and recruit parents to become active participants in their children's literacy development. I would like to thank Lynne Bigelman (Adams Elementary School, Waterford, MI, School District) for sharing authentic examples of how to reach out to families and children. I would like to thank Charline J. Barnes of West Virginia University for the photos she contributed. Also Shera Emmons, a Kindergarten teacher (Discovery Elementary School, Williamston, MI, School District) for allowing me to share her parent newsletter with other teachers. I would like to thank Daymon Hartley (a freelance photographer) and Margaret Trimer-Hartley (Superintendent, University Prep Science & Math, Detroit, MI) for the introductory letter they wrote to their son's Kindergarten teacher. I would also like to thank two of my doctoral students: Rebecca Norman and Autumn Dodge. Rebecca Norman developed all of the charts and graphs for the book and provided helpful feedback and suggestions. Autumn Dodge worked to edit content and provide feedback, resources, and suggestions. There is no way to adequately acknowledge the value and extent of Rebecca and Autumn's contributions. I want to thank two of my former doctoral students (Gwendolyn McMillon, Oakland University, and Jennifer Turner, University of Maryland–College Park) for their encouragement in completing this book as well as their feedback on the manuscript.

I would like to thank my longtime friend and mentor, Dorothy S. Strickland, the Samuel L. Proctor Endowed Chair and the New Jersey Governor's Endowed Chair for writing an excellent foreword. Finally, I want to express my sincere appreciation to my editor, Lois Bridges, who took my ideas and helped me shape them into an informative and useful book for parents, early childhood educators, preservice/inservice teachers, teacher educators, administrators, staff developers, and state department educators. Special thanks to Gloria Pipkin for nudging me for additional detail and clarification and to my development and production editor, Danny Miller, whose copyediting skills are impressive.

Foreword

Tapping the Potential of Parents is an absolute gem. Patricia Edwards has managed successfully to address one of the most important challenges facing educators today—bringing home and school together in a supportive partnership for children. The content is grounded in a strong research base. At the same time, it is practical and highly accessible for busy practitioners.

The link between supportive parental involvement and children's educational development is well established. For example, research has shown that children from homes where parents model the uses of literacy and engage children in activities that promote basic understandings about literacy are better prepared for school and better able to take advantage of what schools have to offer. As Edwards points out, successful parent involvement programs help parents understand the importance of their role as "first teachers" and equip them with skills and strategies to foster their children's ability to take advantage of opportunities to learn.

Effective parent involvement programs also emphasize the importance of the collaborative nature of school and home. In this book, Patricia Edwards helps educators understand the critical role of parents as partners in their efforts. They are reminded that children have lives outside of school that profoundly influence their learning in school.

In a climate where educators often feel overwhelmed by the increasing responsibilities they are asked to undertake, the notion of engaging in parent involvement initiatives may be viewed as another burden added to a heavy load of responsibilities. Fortunately, Edwards has framed the book in a way that emphasizes parent involvement as a "whole school" undertaking that will assist the school community in its goal to help children become successful learners. Educators will find *Tapping the Potential of Parents* to be an excellent resource for fostering a positive school climate, improving relations between home and school, and promoting student achievement.

Dorothy S. Strickland, Ph.D.
Samuel DeWitt Proctor Professor of Education
Rutgers, The State University of New Jersey

Introduction

- Do you organize breakfast meetings, back-to-school nights, carnivals, spaghetti dinners, ice cream socials, Donuts for Dads, and Muffins for Moms events at your school and still feel that you are not adequately reaching the families in your community?

- Do you have parents at your school willing to bring in cupcakes, but when it comes to participating in their children's education, they seem unavailable?

- Do you feel frustrated when parents never return notes, don't answer phone calls, and fail to check their child's homework?

- Do you need help with reexamining your parent-involvement policies and programs?

- Do you want a useful resource with step-by-step guidelines to help you move parent involvement from rhetoric to practice?

Here is an accessible, friendly resource for elementary and middle school teachers, filled with research-based and classroom-tested strategies. Many books have been written on parent involvement, but few have provided a chronology of the "must-do" strategies schools should employ to create an effective and successful family-involvement program.

Of course, I encourage you to deviate from the strategies I recommend. Once you become familiar with the strategies, you will probably want to experiment with and augment these ideas with your own based on your knowledge of your students and their families.

The strategies in this book are presented in chronological order, with step-by-step instructions on how to use each strategy in combination with other classroom/school applications. Strategies are organized into three categories: (1) gathering information about parents and families, (2) analyzing and sharing information with colleagues, and (3) communicating with and recruiting parents.

Key Features

- Strategies are arranged chronologically across the school year.

- A consistent, easy-to-understand format helps you implement each strategy effectively and quickly.

- Applications and examples are included to demonstrate strategies and to stimulate your own creativity.

How to Use This Book

Tapping the Potential of Parents: A Strategic Guide to Boosting Student Achievement Through Family Involvement is a great resource for teachers and administrators who want to learn how to create a working partnership with parents. It can also be used as a supplementary text-book in an educational foundations course, a professional roles and responsibilities course, or any reading, literacy, or language-arts methods course. Coaches and teacher educators will also find it helpful in professional-development workshops and preservice classes.

Chapter 1

Defining Parent/Family Involvement

The word *parent* is used to refer to all those who are involved in a child's education, because we recognize that other adults such as grandparents, aunts, uncles, stepparents, and guardians may carry the primary responsibility for a child's education and development. For our purposes, *parent* includes any adult who plays an important role in a child's upbringing and well-being. *Parent involvement* is the participation of parents in every facet of children's education and development from birth to adulthood, accompanied by the recognition that parents are the primary influence in children's lives.

According to Carol Ascher (1988), the term parent involvement "may easily mean quite different things to different people" (p. 10). In a broad sense, parent involvement includes home-based activities that relate to children's education in school. It can also include school-based activities where the parents actively participate in events that take place during the school day.

Joyce L. Epstein (2001) describes six major levels of involvement:

- **Parenting** includes the basic child-rearing approaches that prepare children for school.

- **Communication** includes effective forms of both home-to-school and school-to-home information-sharing about school programs as well as children's progress.

- **Volunteering** may involve parents who work at the school level, assisting teachers in classrooms. It may also include parental support for their children in extracurricular activities such as sports and fundraising events.

- **Learning at home** includes "requests and guidance from teachers for parents to assist their own children at home on learning activities that are coordinated with the children's classwork" (Epstein, 2001, p. 136).

- **Decision making** includes families involved in school governance and advocacy through school advisory councils, Parent Teacher Associations, and other groups that support and develop parents as leaders and representatives.

- **Collaborating with the community** engages parents in identifying relevant community resources and helping to integrate them in ways that support children's learning and strengthen school programs.

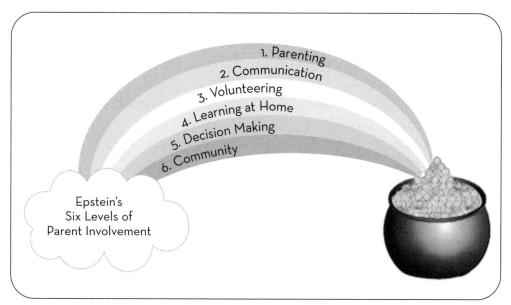

Figure 1.1: Epstein's Six Levels of Parent Involvement

It is important to come to some consensus as to what parent involvement means at your school. In my work with schools throughout the country, I have come to believe that teachers and administrators need to formulate multiple definitions of parent involvement that represent the school's philosophy. It is important that schools develop specific policies about the roles parents may or should assume.

The questions below can help you hone your definitions of parent involvement at the classroom and school level. You may want to discuss these questions with your colleagues:

- What can I do in my school/classroom to promote meaningful parent involvement?

- How should I reorganize my classroom instruction based on what I know about my students' home situations and their parents' abilities to help them?

- What do I need to know so I won't offend parents, particularly parents of minority or immigrant students?

- How should I interact with parents who have an ideology of parent involvement that conflicts with my own expectations?

- When the parents of my students choose not to be involved, should I seek out other family or community members to serve as advocates for these children?

- Do my current parent-involvement practices take into consideration my students' social, emotional, physical, and academic needs? Are my expectations for parent involvement unrealistic based on the families of the children I teach?

How can I begin to rethink in my school/classroom the taken-for-granted, institutionally sanctioned means for teachers and parents to communicate (e.g., PTA meetings, open-house rituals at the beginning of the school year, writing and telephoning parents, and so on)?

The figure on the following page is intended to represent some of the phrases, comments, reflections, and statements that teachers, administrators, researchers, policy makers, parents, and community leaders have used when asked to define or describe parent involvement.

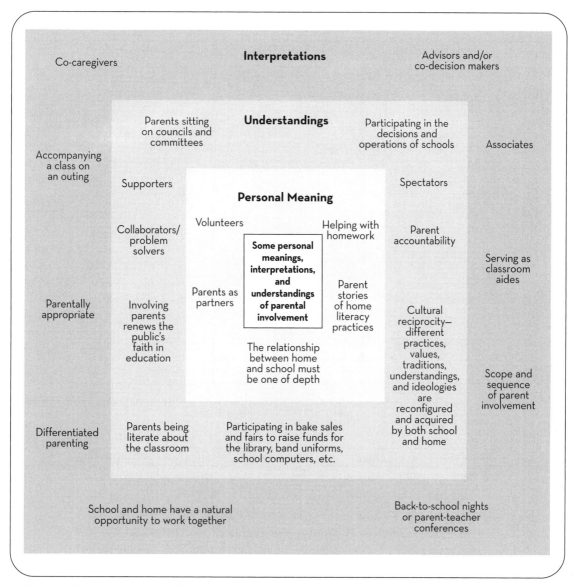

Figure 1.2: *Personal Meanings, Understandings, and Interpretations Associated With Parental Involvement*

Your Definition	Your School's Definition	Conflicts Between Your Definition and the School's Definition

Figure 1.3: Coming to Consensus Around Parent Involvement

In Figure 1.2, I highlighted several personal meanings, interpretations, and understandings associated with parent involvement. I also want to highlight two concepts that I believe schools and teachers can use to build a stronger case for parent involvement. Guofang Li (2006) built on Wendy Winters' (1993) notion of "reciprocal enculturation" and proposed a model of change that she called a pedagogy of cultural reciprocity. In this model, Li suggests that different practices, values, traditions, understandings, and ideologies are reconfigured and acquired by both school and home agencies. Similarly, Lyn Corno (1989) has suggested that students need to be acclimated to the school classroom discourse (as cited in Gee, 1987). By discourse, Gee means "a socially accepted association among ways of using language, of thinking, and of acting that can be used to identify oneself as a member of a socially meaningful group or social network" (as cited in

Mitchell and Weiler, 1991). Gee also suggests that we "think of a discourse as an 'identity kit' which comes complete with the appropriate costume and instructions on how to act and talk so as to take on a particular role that others will recognize." Of course, parents can and should help their children acquire and learn this process. Corno (1989) explains:

The term *classroom literacy* can be used to denote a state of being literate about classrooms. Just as we can be literate about subject matter such as science, art, or history, so we can be literate about events, people, and places like classrooms. Being literate about classrooms means being able to read classrooms as texts. As with any text, the text of a classroom may be read at many levels. Students who are literate about classrooms will 'read' them at a higher semantic level than those who are not (p. 29).

Evaluating Parent Involvement at Your School

All schools should periodically examine their histories to determine if past policies and practices have made parents feel invited or unwelcome. Joyce Epstein (1988) noted that "schools of the same type serve different populations, have different histories of involving parents, and have teachers and administrators with different philosophies, training, and skills in involving parents" (p. 58). Epstein's observation should encourage you to consider a number of questions:

- What is our school's history of involving parents and families?

- What is our school's philosophy regarding parents' involvement in school activities?

- What training and skills do we need for involving parents in school affairs?

One way to begin the process of finding out about your school's history, philosophy, and commitment to parent participation is to complete the profile of parent involvement (see Figure 1.4).

The different roles parents can assume are outlined in this profile; as you'll see, there are multiple roles with varying degrees of parent involvement.

1. *Partners*: Parents meet basic obligations for their child's education and social development.

Profile of Parent Involvement

		Partners	Collaborators and Problem Solvers	Supporters	Advisors and/or Co-Decision Makers	Audience
Ethnicity	African-American					
	Asian					
	Caucasian					
	Hispanic/Latino					
	Native American					
	Other					
Mother's Level of Education	Some High School					
	High School Graduate or Equivalent					
	Some College					
	College Graduate					
	Graduate/Professional Degree					
Father's Level of Education	Some High School					
	High School Graduate or Equivalent					
	Some College					
	College Graduate					
	Graduate/Professional Degree					
Employment	Mother Employed Full-time					
	Mother Employed Part-time					
	Mother Unemployed					
	Father Employed Full-time					
	Father Employed Part-time					
	Father Unemployed					
Lives With	Both Parents					
	Mother					
	Father					
	Other Guardian					
Languages Spoken at Home	English					
Form of Transportation	Bus					
	Walker					
	Drop-off					
	Other					
Free/ Reduced Lunch	Yes					
	No					

Figure 1.4: Profile of Parent Involvement

2. *Collaborators and Problem Solvers*: Parents reinforce the school's efforts with their child and help to solve problems.

3. *Supporters*: Parents provide volunteer assistance to teachers, the parent organization, and to other parents.

4. *Advisors and/or Co-Decision Makers*: Parents provide input on school policy and programs through membership in ad hoc or permanent governance bodies. (Henderson, Marburger & Ooms, 1986, p. 3)

5. *Audience*: Parents attend and appreciate the school's (and their child's) performances and productions.

Many of the parents at your school may not become involved if they do not feel that the school climate—the social and educational atmosphere of the school—is one that makes them feel welcomed, respected, trusted, heard, and needed. See Figure 1.5 and take a few minutes to assess as a staff the parent involvement climate at your school.

Parent Involvement Climate

Present Conditions
Goals
Bridges
Barriers
First Steps

Figure 1.5: Assessing the Parent Involvement Climate

A positive school climate welcomes and encourages family involvement. Family involvement brings about improved teaching: it helps you to generate a positive attitude and raise your self-esteem, and you will feel respected by families who are involved. Improved teaching leads to greater academic achievement by students. Academic achievement and student success lead to a positive school climate. This circular, reciprocal relationship is illustrated below.

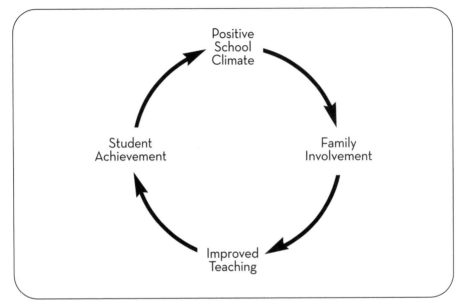

Figure 1.6: Family Involvement Leads to Student Achievement

Next Steps

- Take a few minutes to write down your definition of what parent involvement means to you as a classroom teacher, and what it means at your school.
- Share your thoughts with your grade-level colleagues.
- Are there any conflicts between your beliefs about parent involvement and what your school believes?

Remember, it is important to come to some consensus as to what involvement means at your school. Once you do this, you are well on your way to restructuring the ways you will work with parents.

Chapter 2

Creating a Welcoming Environment for Parents

Most parents want to be supportive of their children and to participate in their children's educational success. Participation will mean different things to different parents but may include:

- Establishing a comfortable relationship with their child's teacher.

- Knowing when and how they can get in touch with the teacher especially if their child is having a problem.

- Understanding the teacher's program and her academic and behavioral expectations.

- Acknowledging the school and district standards and curricular guidelines.

- Understanding how and when they might volunteer in the classroom or help with special school events.

- Working with their children at home, monitoring their homework, and helping as needed in appropriate ways.

It is the school's responsibility to figure out how to welcome parents into the educational process. Increasingly, you are likely to have parents in your school who speak languages other than English. The families at your school may have had different, few, or no experience with formal education. You might be serving parents who are immigrants undergoing cultural dissonance and acculturation. Consequently, they bring new approaches and challenges to school. They especially must feel welcome and invited. What follows are simple but effective ideas you might try.

Create Welcoming Signs or Banners

It is extremely important to develop a welcoming environment in your

Figure 2.1

school and classroom for parents and family members. When parents enter the school building they need to feel comfortable. According to Purkey and Novak (1984), schools should be "the most inviting place in town" (p. 2). One easy way to create a warm, inclusive school environment is to post welcoming banners or signs in a prominent location near the entrance of the school so that when parents step inside they feel immediately "at home." Consider creating welcoming signs in the various languages spoken by the families in your school.

Create Eye-Catching Bulletin Boards

Taking a tip from Shelley Harwayne, the award-winning former principal of the Manhattan New School (who went on to become the award-winning superintendent of District No. 2), turn your bulletin boards into information-rich centers for parents and visitors to your school or classroom. As Harwayne makes clear in her seminal work, *Going Public: Priorities and Practice at the Manhattan New School* (Heinemann, 1999), bulletin boards are an easy and very public way to share the school's interests, talents, priorities, teaching strategies, and the powerful work in which all members of the school community are engaged day in and day out. Teachers can also use them to invite parent participation. Following Harwayne's lead, encourage parents to send in a favorite photo or illustration of their family engaged in a "literacy event"—reading aloud letters from relatives, snuggling in bed with a bedtime story, or a playing a rollicking game of Boggle—together with a caption that explains what's taking place in the photograph. Post these photographs and captions on the bulletin boards at the school's entrance or along the hallways to create an instant sense of home-school community. Parents who enter a school and see such rich family-oriented displays receive an immediate and powerful message: "You are welcome in our school!"

Figure 2.2: Parent Bulletin Boards (photos by Charline J. Barnes)

Create a Parent Bulletin Board

Over the years, many of you may have designed bulletin boards that welcome students to school and set the tone for learning. These bulletin boards can also serve as a welcome for parents and a place for important parent information and announcements.

In general, bulletin boards help establish a positive climate in your classroom and school. A bulletin board is a way to:

- get a message across visually

- add visual interest and color to a setting

- attract attention to an idea

- teach and reinforce learning

- say something important without being wordy

- start people thinking, wondering, and questioning

Recognize that bulletin boards are an important element in the school that speak to all parents—from kindergarten to high school. But no matter what the grade level, bulletin boards have little value unless they attract the parents' and students' attention.

Welcome to Our School

List of Teachers and Support Staff	Monthly School Calendar	Major School Events for Entire Year	Television Programs or Movies That Families May Enjoy
School Event Notice	PTA/PTO Sponsored Event Notice	Upcoming Community Events for Families	Classroom Norms and Expectations
Daily Lunch Menu	Next PTA Meeting	Parent Sign-Up Sheet	Handbook of School Policies and Programs *(Please pick up in the main office if you did not receive one at open house.)*

Figure 2.3: Example of Content for Parent Bulletin Boards

Send Welcoming Letters to Parents

Many teachers now routinely write a welcome letter to parents at the beginning of the school year or when a new student enrolls. If possible, draw on your school's diverse community to find translators who can help write the letter in the different languages that are represented in your classroom. These letters may provide a relatively brief welcome and include bulleted information about the school year ahead or they may unfold over several pages and feature personal details about you as a teacher. In the letter at right, meet Becky Johnson, a second grade teacher in Norwalk, Connecticut. See how she shares information about herself as well as her program and includes key information about the supplies students need.

A grade-level group of teachers may choose to work together in crafting a common letter to parents. On the next page is a letter from a group of kindergarten teachers that focuses on how school and home can work together in supporting emergent literacy.

Sample letter from second grade teacher

Dear Parents,

Welcome to Room 114! I am very excited to be your child's second grade teacher, and I would like to introduce myself.

I grew up in Simsbury, Connecticut, and currently live in Norwalk. In 1999, I graduated from Bucknell University with a B.S. in Elementary Education. I then attended Ohio State University where I received my Master's in Literacy in 2000. This year will be my fifth year at Ridgefield. I taught third grade for three years before moving to second grade last year. I really enjoyed the change in grades and am looking forward to the coming year.

We will have a busy year ahead of us. In math, we will be focusing on addition and subtraction of single and multiple digit numbers, measurement, geometric shapes, graphing, and fractions. For reading, students are encouraged to choose their own just-right books as they learn to read more fluently, continue to study word-attack skills, and further develop their comprehension. Science and social studies will allow us to explore the depths of the ocean, the habits and habitats of local animals, all seven continents, the lives of Native Americans (both past and present), and to go back in time to when the dinosaurs lived. Many of our projects will not be possible without parent participation. At Open House, I will give you more information about these volunteer opportunities, and I hope you will be able to participate.

I believe that home-school communication is extremely important. Because of this, you will receive a Friday's Eye on Room 114 at the end of most weeks. I ask that you review these newsletters with your child, and sign and return the bottom portion each Monday. There will be a section for your comments and questions, as well. Also, please feel free to email (bjohnson@ridgefield.edu) or call me (555-9764) at school, if you have any questions or comments.

Finally, enclosed you will find information regarding our specials (music, art, library, and physical education) schedule, a list of school supplies, and a parent survey. Nobody knows your child better than you. Therefore, I ask that you fill out the survey, adding any additional information you think I should know, and return with your child on the first week of school. This will help me get to know your child.

I look forward to working with you and your child this year.

Sincerely,

Becky Johnson

Sample letter from group of Kindergarten teachers

Dear Families,

During this important year of kindergarten, you will notice many positive changes in your child. Your child is becoming more independent, making new friends, and learning new skills at school. A natural skill your child will continue to develop is Emergent Literacy. Emergent Literacy is a continual progression of a young learner's **reading**, **writing**, **listening**, and **speaking ability**.

Oral language is continually modeled for young children; what's more, they are actively involved in learning how to talk, trying out new words and experimenting with different styles and structures. Children need to learn written language in the same interactive way they learn oral language. Books and real-life experiences help make oral and written language meaningful. Other valuable everyday experiences include being read to, imitating reading and writing, noticing signs around the school and community, and writing familiar names.

Learning to read is connected to learning to write. We can view children's writing as a progression from pictures and symbols to more formal writing (see Emergent Writing Processes page). Children are learning that writing has meaning and that their thoughts and ideas can be shared in a different ways. Here are some helpful materials that we suggest you might provide at home.

- **Paper**: different sizes and shapes, lined and unlined, colored and white, envelopes, greeting cards, memo pads, post-it notes, stamps, and a recycle box
- **Writing utensils**: pencils, crayons, markers, pens, and colored pencils
- **Other supplies**: stamps, stamp pads, scissors, rulers, stapler, a copy of the alphabet, and a list of student names in the class

Children are also involved in a natural progression when learning to read. You may see some of these traits as your child is developing emergent reading skills.

- Holding the book right side up
- Turning the pages from left to right
- Knowing the words on the page contain meaning
- Making connections between the illustrations and words
- Telling the story in their own words
- Memorizing part of the story to retell
- Responding to books containing rhyme and repetition

When you read to your child, you are providing them with a model of what readers do and are demonstrating a purpose for reading. The many benefits children gain from being read to include:

- increasing his or her vocabulary
- improving his or her knowledge of story structure
- valuing reading
- increasing his or her listening skills
- finding pleasure in reading

Children will construct their own ideas about reading and writing gradually. The speed at which they

(continued on next page)

progress is influenced by environmental factors. These factors include the amount of time they experience reading and writing in the home, how much support they feel, how safe they feel to try something new, and being engaged in meaningful reading and writing activities at school.

You can trust that we will promote Emergent Literacy in the classroom. The following are some ways we will foster reading, writing, speaking, and listening skills.

- We will engage children in stories including big books, books with repetition, informational stories, and quality children's literature.

- We will have purposeful writing activities including letters to friends, writing to reinforce new lessons, and journal writing.

- There will be independent reading and writing activities around the room during center time.

- We will encourage active listening and meaningful questioning skills during sharing time.

It is our plan to create a good foundation for your child and to continue the progression of literacy. It is important that we work together, as partners, at home and at school. The following are some ways you can continue literacy progression at home.

- Read with your child.
  — Ask your child questions about the story.
  — Make connections between illustration and text, self and text, text and text, and world and text.
  — Praise the efforts your child makes.
  — Take several trips to a library or book store.

- Enjoy trips to the grocery store (or any other store).
  — Observe street signs along the way.
  — Notice the store name.
  — Look for specific ingredients in a recipe.
  — Check the prices.
  — Identify brand names.
  — Check items off the shopping list.

- Write letters or birthday cards to friends and relatives.

- Let your child help you follow a recipe and cook.

Research indicates that children who are read to regularly by parents, siblings, or other individuals in the home become early readers and show a natural interest in books. We are interested in the ways you promote literacy at home and would appreciate it if you would like to share some of your ideas with us.

We would like to thank you for your assistance in these areas as together we help support your child while he or she progresses through Emergent Literacy!

Sincerely,

Kindergarten Teachers

Communicate Through Parent Newsletters

In addition to writing a beginning-of-the-school-year welcoming letter, many teachers find it helpful to communicate with their parents via a weekly, bimonthly, or monthly newsletter. Depending on the community in which you teach and the resources your parents have, you may find it easier to rely on email, a classroom blog, or other electronic means of communication. The example on the next page shows a more traditional newsletter from Shera Emmons' primary classroom. Note how she combines news about her curriculum and classroom events with hints for parental participation and support.

Create "What We Learned" Storybooks

One of the best ways to reach out to parents is to share the work that you're doing in your classroom. In addition to the traditional Back-to-School and Open House events that typically include rich displays of student work, make sure you find ways to routinely send your students' work home in ways that invite parents to notice, interact with, and respond to their students and to you. One simple but effective way to accomplish this goal is to create student-authored "What We Learned" storybooks that detail and present student learning as part of a content-area study, field trip, or presentation from an outside visitor. Each student may write his or her own book as part of "What I Learned" self-reflection, or you might prefer to create a class book as an overarching review of a whole classroom learning experience. Either way, students take their books home with letters to their families explaining that the book's purpose provides them with an opportunity to share and discuss their learning. They read the books aloud to family members and then engage in conversations about what they learned. Family members sign off after they've read the book and add any comments they'd like to make. Students are invited to share the book with as many family members as possible—friends and neighbors, too—and have everyone add thoughts, comments, and questions to the comments page.

Sample newsletter

Dear Families:

It is September! We've had an exciting first few weeks of school. Here is an update of the happenings in our room and some important dates:

August 20th—Ryan's birthday!

September 5th—Cami's birthday

September 15th—Picture Day

September 21st—Student Membership Count Day

September 22nd—PTA Welcome Back Night/Book Fair (5 pm–8:30 pm)

September 23rd—Book Fair (8:30 am–12:00 pm)

Please remember that if you would like your child to have milk at snack time, you need to buy it through the office. You can pay for it for the year or half the year. You can call Denise Williams in the office for more information.

Everyone has been doing a great job of checking and returning the purple notes folders! Remember to check your child's backpack for the folder on Tuesdays and Fridays and return it with any notes for me.

Thanks!

Aug. 29–Sept. 1:	Aa
Sept. 6–9:	Mm
Sept. 12–16:	Bb
Sept. 19–23:	Ss
Sept. 26–30:	Pp

Math:

We are practicing counting, identifying, and writing numbers. Currently, our focus is 0 through10, but we do work with larger numbers every day at calendar time. Our goal by the end of the year is for your child to be able to read and write the numbers to 30. We have spent some time exploring materials we will be using when we investigate math. Ask your child about the geo blocks, pattern blocks, and the jumbo pattern blocks!

Global Studies:

We are learning how to interact peacefully with our classmates by practicing our respectful listening skills. We are working hard at raising a quiet hand when we have an idea to share. We are beginning to discuss our three rules for the classroom:

- We are all here to learn.
- We learn best when we feel happy and safe.
- We will help each other learn a little every day.

Baby News:

My family and I are excited to announce that we are expecting a new addition to our family! As many of you already know, I am pregnant. Baby Emmons is due on November 8th. We are working hard to find the best possible teacher to take over while I am on maternity leave. Thanks for all of your support during this exciting time!

Please feel free to contact me if you have any questions or thoughts. Email is a great way to get a hold of me because I usually check my email from home. If you'd like to speak to me directly, my planning time is from 9:20–9:50 every day, and I'm usually at school all day on Tuesdays. Have a great weekend!

Mrs. Shera Emmons

[include email and phone number]

I am still missing several Field Trip Permission Slips. I need to have one on file for everyone, even if we are just taking a walk trip. I will always notify you ahead of time if we are going to leave school property. If you need another copy, please let me know.

Book Order:

Attached is this month's book order. The book orders are an excellent opportunity to help encourage your developing reader at reasonable prices. Plus, every dollar spent earns our class points to use toward free books. Please return your orders by this Friday (September 9th). If you decide to order, please fill out the provided order forms and make one check out to Scholastic Book Clubs for the total amount of all your orders. Do not make out checks to the school. Return both the order form and check in a labeled envelope to me. The orders take about two weeks to come in once placed.

Sharing:

Please look at the September sharing schedule to find your child's special sharing day. (Let me know if you need another copy.) Please help your child prepare to talk about his or her item, as well as answer three questions from his or her classmates. We have discussed

that a question is something you are wondering about, or more information you would like to know. On Fridays, everyone is invited to bring in an object that starts with our focus letter of the week. We will be comparing the different objects as a group.

Literacy:

Students have the opportunity to read books every day. Sometimes I will read to them, other times they will share the reading, chiming in when they discover the pattern. Also, each week they will be illustrating and reading a letter book. Please ask your child to read it to you when they bring it home. Encourage them to use the pictures to help them decode the words. Applaud every good attempt. We are growing readers!

We discuss every letter every day, but each week has a different focus letter, which drives some of our activities for the week. My goal is for your child to be able to identify every letter by sight and sound and write each letter by the end of the school year. Below are the focus letters for September:

Sample RealeBook

I like to read
with my mom.

Me gusta leer
con mi mama.

PARENT PAGE

Four Ways to Help Your Child Learn How to Read

- Find time to read together each day.
- Make a special place to keep your child's books.
- Talk about what you read.
- Relax and have fun!

RealeBooks ("Really Books") makes it especially easy to create digital picture books online. Students and teachers can download and print beautiful quality picture books for side-by-side sharing; they can also email the books to family members at home or anywhere in the world, or post them to a school-wide digital library for later viewing. Visit www.realebooks.com to learn how your school can create a network of home/school correspondence through individual books, as well as an electronic library that showcases all the school-created books. RealeBooks invites comments and parent participation; indeed, the books for the younger children often end with a "Parent Page," a special set of simple directions to encourage parents to read aloud to their children.

Create a Parent Survey

Nearly all schools recognize the value of a parent survey—a quick and effective way to gather valuable information about a student's family members, contact information, schedules, and the like. With this information in hand, you can schedule your parent conferences at a workable time for students' parents making it more likely that they will be able to attend.

Parent and Student Information

Child's name: _____

Mother's name: _____

Father's name: _____

Address: _____

_____

Phone: _____

Best time to call or visit your home: _____

Father's occupation: _____

Mother's occupation: _____

Best day and time for parents to attend sessions: _____

Comments: _____

_____

Figure 2.4: Sample Form for Parent and Student Information

Conduct a School Climate Assessment Survey

Creating a warm, family-friendly atmosphere doesn't have to be costly, complicated, or time-consuming. When parents feel welcome, it can make a significant and rewarding difference to all involved. Interviews with parents, business leaders, community members, and others reveal that certain characteristics common among schools are regarded as welcoming. Use the following School Climate Assessment Survey to determine if such characteristics are present at your school. Use the survey and the subsequent suggestions as a thought-provoking tool to determine how to create a positive, welcoming, family-friendly environment for the students, teachers, and parents at your school. Answer the following questions regarding the level of family-friendliness at your school and in your classroom.

School Climate Assessment Survey

Exterior and Grounds

yes no

- ☐ ☐ Are there signs on the main roads that direct you to the school? Are the signs clearly visible with large print?
- ☐ ☐ Once on school grounds, are there signs directing you to visitor parking, or parent parking? Are there clearly marked spaces for disabled parking? Are there signs that indicate where buses will be arriving and departing?
- ☐ ☐ Are the grounds and parking lots free of litter, debris, and/or unsightly weeds? Is there a garden, flowerbed, or other landscaping on the property?
- ☐ ☐ Are there pictures (such as the school mascot), banners, flags, etc. that show school spirit posted around the school? Are there signs that support character education, diversity, or other messages from student groups?
- ☐ ☐ Is the main entrance of the building well marked and obvious? Are all other doors marked "Please use main entrance"? Does the building look well secured?
- ☐ ☐ What adjectives would you use to describe the overall appearance of the building and grounds? What kind of image is reflected or expressed?

Interior

yes no

- ☐ ☐ Is there a security sign directing all visitors to report to the office upon entering? Is there also a sign letting parents know they are welcome (e.g., "ABC School Welcomes Parents")?
- ☐ ☐ Are there welcome signs/materials translated into appropriate languages?
- ☐ ☐ Are there introductory tours/presentations made?
- ☐ ☐ Are there special events used to introduce new arrivals to special people such as the principal and teachers?
- ☐ ☐ Are there clear directions to the office? Is the office door clearly marked?
- ☐ ☐ Are the school's mission statement, vision statement, and/or core values (indicating a commitment to the community it serves) prominently posted near the entrance?
- ☐ ☐ Is someone available to greet visitors if they need to wait on a student or teacher? Are there parent educational materials on display in the waiting area? Is information about PTA/PTO or Boosters' groups available with dates/times of meetings, names of officers, and contact information?
- ☐ ☐ Are the hallways clean, quiet, and free of litter? Does the school's appearance reflect an orderly and safe environment conducive to effective learning and productivity?
- ☐ ☐ What kinds of items are displayed throughout the school, in hallways, and on bulletin boards? What do these items tell you about the academic environment of the school?
- ☐ ☐ What kind of adjectives would you use to describe the interior of the school? What kind of image is reflected or expressed? Are these images also expressed in your classroom?

School Faculty, Staff, and Students

yes no

- ☐ ☐ Do school faculty, staff (including secretaries, custodians, bus drivers, and so on), and students show respectful and courteous behavior toward all visitors?
- ☐ ☐ Do school faculty and staff set good examples for students by demonstrating kindness and good manners toward each other as well as visitors?
- ☐ ☐ Do school faculty and staff convey an interest in students' futures?
- ☐ ☐ Does school faculty welcome volunteers in their classrooms?
- ☐ ☐ Does school faculty accept accountability for students' performance?
- ☐ ☐ Does school faculty exhibit high-quality teaching and professionalism?
- ☐ ☐ Does school faculty interact well with parents?
- ☐ ☐ Does school faculty show a willingness to provide extra help to students who need it?
- ☐ ☐ Does school faculty show a willingness to help parents help their students?
- ☐ ☐ Are you satisfied with your school's performance on the climate survey? If yes, keep up the good work. If not, get started.

Post Your School's Mission Statement for Parent Involvement

What is your school's mission statement and how does it relate to your students' families? If it doesn't exist or you can't recall it, it's time to take another look. A mission statement can be a focal point for learning. It can guide all school activities and even assist you in choosing the right people to join your staff. The clearer a school community is about its mission statement, the more successful it can be. A mission can serve as a centerpiece for faculty, staff, parents, and students. It can serve as a framework for making decisions and for building relationships. Powerful missions give people a sense of purpose and passion. Every school should crisply articulate a mission statement and walk the talk. I have included four examples of mission statements.

Sample mission statements

Our vision is to provide each student a diverse education in a safe, supportive environment that promotes self-discipline, motivation, and excellence in learning.

The mission of Turner Elementary School is to provide an individualized, nurturing educational foundation and enable all students to become intellectually competent, responsible citizens and productive learners and workers who can compete confidently in a dynamic global society.

Our vision is for parents to partner together with staff and administration to make the elementary years as meaningful as possible. We know how children benefit from parent involvement. We also know how valuable time is these days, and so the more concerned adults that come forward, the better. Besides, it's fun!

Our vision is to become an excellent school without sacrificing our academic standards; to create a safe and enjoyable environment for faculty, staff, and students; and to provide a well-rounded education both academically and socially for all students. We plan to accomplish these goals by providing our students with many opportunities to develop their academic and social skills through the use of innovative teaching strategies and continual assessment. This plan will help us to identify their interests and special talents and develop a sense of belonging. Through new, innovative programs and an enthusiastic and caring staff, this vision will become a reality for teachers, parents, and students.

What is your school's mission? Is it reflected in your classroom? If not, begin working to align your school/classroom mission.

Steps to Composing a School Mission Statement

Use this template to create a draft of your school's mission statement.

1. Brainstorm 3-5 ideas you think are key to providing a good education for all students.

2. Using your ideas, write a draft of your school's mission statement on the back of this paper.

3. Compare your mission statements to those of your colleagues.
   - What do the statements have in common?
   - How are they different?
   - How can you combine your ideas to make one cohesive mission statement for your school?

4. Write a final mission statement.

Figure 2.5

Encourage Parents and Students to Create Vision Statements

A parent vision survey, an extension of the more basic parent survey, is one way to get insightful information about a parent's vision of school success. Parents know their children best, are in the best position to inform the school about their children's needs and capacities, and are deeply invested in their children's success. (See Figure 2.6 on the next page for an example of a parent survey.)

Parents who support their children's academic achievement often hold powerful visions of school success. So much of what happens in a family's household depends on them. That's why the exercise of having parents write a vision statement is so powerful. It provides the opportunity for parents to define their family's vision of academic achievement and literacy development, and to describe the interactions they want to build. Keep in mind, too, that there is no "wrong" way of doing this. In addition, as you have parents work through this exercise, try to keep their minds focused on what they want for their children's future; they don't have to limit themselves to what is happening now or what has taken place in the past. You can encourage parents to revise their vision statement several times a year and make changes to reflect new values, hopes, and dreams.

I also think that it is a great idea to have both older and younger students write a vision statement of education. What's good about doing this? Well, you will have the opportunity to compare the information found in parent and student vision statements. I have included three different forms to assist you in helping parents and students to get started writing their vision statements. If parents have difficulty writing their responses, you have the option of tape recording their responses. This could be a task for the home-school-community liaison. You will also need to make an extra effort to collect a vision statement from parents and students who speak languages other than English or may speak several English dialects.

Parent Vision Survey

Please fill out this parent survey about your child and return on the first day of school. This information will be kept confidential.

Child's name _____

Parents' names _____

Best number to reach you _____

Email address _____

Does your child have siblings? Please list their names and ages

_____

_____

_____

What does your child like to do with his or her free time?

What you do you like to do as a family?

What are your child's strengths?

What are your child's needs?

Additional information:

Thank you for your help!

Figure 2.6

Parent's Vision for Child's Education

Please think about your vision for your child's education. Write a few sentences in response to each of these questions.

What is your vision for your child's classroom? (What would you like your child's classroom to look like? How is the classroom set up? How is the classroom decorated? What is the teacher doing? What are the students doing?)

What is your vision for your role in your child's education?

What is your vision for your child as a student?

What is your vision for your child's future?

Figure 2.7

Older Child's Vision of Education

Please think about your vision for your education. Write a few sentences in response to each of these questions.

What is your vision for your classroom? (What would you like your classroom to look like? How is the classroom set up? How is the classroom decorated? What is the teacher doing? What are the students doing?)

What is your vision of your parents' role in your education? (How should your parents help you with school?)

What is your vision for yourself as a student? (How should you act?)

What is your vision for your future? (What do you want to do when you are older? What do you need to do to become that?)

Figure 2.8

Younger Child's Vision of Education

Draw a picture of your classroom.

Draw a picture of your parents helping you learn.

Draw a picture of how you look as a student.

Draw a picture of what you want to be when you grow up.

Figure 2.9

I was touched when a mother who was part of a series of Early Reading First parent workshops I conducted tearfully made this statement:

> "I did not do a good job with my 12-year-old daughter. I rarely helped her with her homework. I didn't like teachers telling me that I should help her at home. I thought that was something that teachers were paid to do—help their students. After attending these workshops, I have come to understand that I was wrong, and I did not have a vision of how my daughter would succeed in school. I needed to change what was happening in my household. With my five-year-old son, I am going to work harder to make sure he does better in school. Parents must have a vision of school success for their own children. I cannot leave that totally up to the teacher."

I hope that this mother holds on to her vision of making changes in her home for her son and moves toward building a vision of what she can do to help her daughter. I'm sure you agree that teachers in schools where parents are actively involved find that their jobs become easier. Working in partnership with students and parents creates an environment of trust, positive interactions, and optimism for what can be accomplished. Having the support of parents relieves considerable stress for teachers who often feel they are struggling alone to improve children's achievement. Effective parent-involvement programs can prevent burnout and the loss of hardworking, dedicated teachers.

Additional Strategies for Making Parents Feel Welcome

Gayle Morrison, a Nationally Board Certified first grade teacher, shares unique ways to connect with teachers (Manning, Morrison, and Camp, 2009). As Gayle notes, "Parents benefit when we involve them intimately in the life of the classroom, because then they have a purpose for becoming involved in their child's education. They see the classroom as belonging to them as well as to their children—and that involvement, of course, benefits their children and their children's teachers as well.

Wanted Posters and Guest Expert Days

Gayle develops home-school relationships through something she calls wanted posters. These posters, drawn by the students, are a clever way to attract experts among the parents who would be willing to visit the class, share their expertise with the students, and, in this way, enrich the curriculum and contribute to the classroom community. Gayle is always amazed and delighted with the numbers of experts in her classrooms. Examples of experts who have visited Gayle's classroom include nurses, firemen, policemen, ministers, teachers, homemakers, chefs, and zoo workers.

All of these experts contribute to the classroom curriculum by sharing their expertise on the three Guest Expert Days scheduled throughout the year. After a parent/community expert visits the classroom, a student committee publishes a book about the visit and places it in the classroom library. The student authors autograph a copy of the original book and give it to the expert as a special thank you for their time.

Traveling Friends

Students can check out one of the 15 traveling friends for a week. The traveling friends might include favorite book characters Clifford, Arthur, D.W., Strega Nona, Corduroy, Berenstain Bears, Lily, Sylvester, Madeline, Frog and Toad, or Olivia, among others. Each friend has a book, a journal, and an activity that parents can do with their child. The students record daily what happens while the traveling friend is visiting. Parents and other family members write in the journals, too; together they enjoy:

- Writing a story about their favorite character in the book.
- Drawing pictures showing the sequence of the story.
- Making a puppet and retelling the story.

At the end of the week, parents are asked to come to school and share the book and activity with the other students. This is always a highlight of the week.

Traveling Science Boxes

Inside tin lunch boxes, parents will find everything they need to perform an experiment with their child based on an appropriate science topic the children are studying in the classroom. Science boxes typically include a book about the science topic and a journal for daily notations about the experiment.

Once the science project is completed, the parents visit the classroom so the student and parent can share the outcome with the entire class. There are five lunch boxes with the same experiment so different outcomes might be shared each Friday, giving the students and parents a chance to discuss and wonder and ask new questions. These five science boxes rotate throughout the year and feature different concepts. It is fascinating to hear parents talk about the experiments and the problems they encounter along the way. It's also great fun listening to the "wows" and the "a-ha's" that occur, and often the parents are more excited about the experiment outcome than the students.

Parent Bags

Gayle designs "Parent Bags" as a tool to give parents additional information and activities to help their children build reading and writing skills at home. In Gayle's weekly newsletter, she introduces the different parent bags that are available for checkout. Parents can check out one of the five bags for a two-week period of time simply by sending in a note with their child requesting a particular bag.

Inside the bag are booklets for parents from the International Reading Association that explain how to help their child become a better reader and writer. Also, there are lists of great read-alouds that can be checked out from the public library. Jim Trelease's Read Aloud Handbook (2001) is also in the bag to give parents suggestions about reading aloud at home. Gayle includes parenting magazines and party idea books, as well as a notebook in which parents write what they liked about the bag and offer suggestions about what to add to the bag to make it more useful for them.

Author Teas

Three times a year, Gayle's class holds an author's tea when parents are invited to hear published works by the classroom authors. The books that are shared all become part of the classroom library. Classroom authors added anywhere from 60 to 100 fiction pieces and at least 30 books a year to their nonfiction library.

The three teas are held before winter break, before spring break, and at the end of the year. The tea before the winter break focuses on seasonal books and stories. The tea before spring break focuses on research projects and student-written nonfiction books that become part of the nonfiction library, available to other students in the school as a resource. At this tea the students walk their parents through the publishing process, showing them their research notes, rough drafts, revisions, and edits made along the way to their finished research report. Parents are impressed to see the amount of learning that takes place while the students are immersed in this process. The final tea is a celebration of all the publications throughout the year.

Form Parent Focus Groups

The parent focus group meeting is an opportunity for parents to voice their opinions on a variety of issues. It's a public forum. Parents can talk about what's on their minds. You can learn about some of the political undercurrents that might be occurring at your school. In particular you can find out from families what they need, what they desire for their children, and how they feel about activities that are in the planning stages.

How to Set Up and Monitor an Effective Parent Focus Group

Preparation

- Arrange chairs in circular formation for approximately ten participants in each group, one facilitator, and one note-taker (size of circle will vary, of course, depending on the number of parents who participate).

- Have name tags and markers available for people to write their names; also include chart paper for the note-taker.

- Greet focus-group participants as they enter the room. If possible, have snacks available (especially important if parents are coming straight from work) and allow time for mingling and socializing.

Introduction

(10 minutes)

Introduce yourself and your colleagues and explain how the focus group will work. Remind parents that there are no right or wrong answers; the goal is to encourage open, honest communication and to share in a warm, encouraging climate their questions, concerns, and hopes for their children's educational experience at your school.

Focus-Group Questions

(30 minutes)

Be sure that you and your colleagues have carefully considered and written out the key questions you'll ask parents to discuss, debate, and question. You might post the questions for all to see or make them available on handouts; ideally, parents have had a chance to review the questions before the meeting so they arrive having thought about their own opinions and questions, and ready to actively engage with the other parents.

Wrap-Up Questions

(20 minutes)

Give each parent an index card and a pen. Ask each parent to write the most important thing they learned and how they might choose to act on their new information. Then ask the parents to share their responses aloud and invite further discussion. Make sure the notes are collected, collated, and written up in a Word document that can be disseminated to the entire school community. As appropriate, draw up an action plan to address the parents' concerns and suggestions.

Parent focus groups also provide an excellent venue for the staff to voice concerns and opinions. I don't have to remind you that there are many problems in today's schools. It has been customary to blame the schools for every problem that crosses their threshold. Most of you would agree that although schools need to be held accountable for their students' progress and success, partnerships with parents are essential to achieving the success of children. Parents need to be held accountable for the academic well-being of their children, just as much, if not more so, than our schools. You might be asking yourself, "How do we do that?" I suggest that you have a parent focus group discussion on parenting contracts and classroom contracts. I also suggest that your school begin asking parents to sign a parenting contract. However, I suggest that before you convene the parent focus group, you meet as a faculty to make sure all of you are on the same page so that the focus group meeting runs smoothly.

Next Steps

- Call a faculty meeting to discuss if the school has done all it can do to welcome a variety of parents in your community (e.g., parents who speak languages other than English, immigrant families, minority families, rural families, and so on).

- If there is some disagreement among your colleagues about how the school is welcoming different family configurations, discuss a plan for addressing the situation.

- Make a concerted effort to encourage all of your colleagues to create parent bulletin boards and to write a welcoming letter to parents as well as ongoing parent newsletters.

Remember to conduct a school climate assessment survey and organize parent focus groups so that you have a sense of how parents feel about your school. Once you have this information, you will have a better grasp on how to serve all of the families in your school community.

Chapter 3

Addressing Challenges Faced by Your Students' Families

Student Mobility

Is student mobility an issue at your school? If not, it could become an issue as your school population changes. The freedom to move and seek new opportunities is a hallmark of our identity as Americans. However, while this freedom may be perceived as a birthright, mobility has its liabilities, especially when it comes to schooling.

Student mobility refers to the phenomenon of students changing schools for reasons other than grade promotion. Student mobility is a topic that frequently surfaces in discussions about the problems of urban and rural schooling. Surprisingly, it tends to fade from the agenda as discussion turns toward reform initiatives and school restructuring (Kerbow, 1996). You will probably agree that students who transfer frequently between schools during the school year are at greater risk for academic and behavioral problems (Hartman, 2002). The face of student mobility is varied. It includes:

- children of families in the military
- children whose families are migrant workers

- children who experience great poverty
- children experiencing homelessness
- children in foster care
- children whose families are struggling with domestic violence, emotional disorders, or substance abuse
- immigrants
- runaways
- "third culture kids" (i.e., students whose parents are from the United States, but whose jobs result in their children being raised and educated in other countries)

(Popp, 2004, p. 2)

Use the table below to examine student mobility in your school district, school, or classroom.

Who?	Factors?	Characteristics/Needs

Adapted from Popp, P.A., Stronge, J.H,. & Hindman, J. (2003)

Figure 3.1: Student Mobility Table

Questions That School Districts Can Ask About Student Mobility

- How much mobility is being experienced across the district/schools?
- What is the impact of high mobility on schools?
- Who is highly mobile?
- Why are students leaving and where are they going?
- When are the children coming into the school? Beginning of school or midyear?
- Why are students arriving and from where?
- Are there identifiable patterns of mobility?
- Who needs the data on mobility?
- What communications vehicles are best for sharing information with target audiences?

How Districts and Schools Can Help Highly Mobile Students

All educators recognize the challenges students face when they are forced, because of economic issues or family challenges, to enter and exit multiple schools—sometimes over the course of one school year. It's nearly impossible to avoid "failure to thrive in school." Students are confused by new curricular programs, overwhelmed by new teachers and classmates, and miss significant chunks of "in-school time" as their family makes the physical move across a city or sometimes to a state on the other side of the country. Moving during the school year and having to change schools is disruptive, and sadly, often destroys the child's chance for school success.

Educators can make a big difference in the lives of these families. Once you suspect a child may have been subjected to frequent moves, you can take steps to help him adjust. First, make sure you record as much information as possible about his transfer if he's leaving your school and moving to another; or conversely, get in touch with the old school and request the child's full set of medical and academic records. You can also check to see if Title I funds can be used to help ease mobile students' transitions from school to school.

Be particularly cautious about special placements such as special education and unique arrangements related to disciplinary actions; you don't want the child to arrive at another school with a cloud hanging over him— especially if the decisions that led to these actions were not sound.

- Track the progress, especially of transient students, who may have already moved repeatedly, and make sure they receive necessary additional assistance; if possible, provide special tutoring to help highly mobile children catch up with the rest of the class.

- Create a plan as a staff for helping mobile students transition more easily; to the extent that you're able, work to develop relationships with the parents and help make them part of the team that oversees and monitors the child's well-being and academic support.

- Counsel parents on the effects moving from school to school has on their children; address this with great sensitivity; poor families are often forced to move their families as their opportunities for work shift to new locations.

- Draw on community resources for additional support such as agencies that deal with housing, utilities, and human and social service; some educators find ways to bring these services directly to the school making it easier for parents with limited means and time.

School-Level Practices That Help Ease the Transition for Highly Mobile Students

- Have a plan in place for handling transfers so the process can unfold in a predictable, nondisruptive manner minimizing the emotional impact of the change all parties involved face.

- Involve translators and counselors, to the extent that it's possible, when registering a new student; again, such personal contact and conversation in the family's native language helps the family feel welcome and cared for and reassures parents that their child will be safely assimilated into the school.

- Follow up with parents several weeks after enrollment. Parents may have questions once their child has started school and may be hesitant to return to school for answers and additional guidance.

- Find ways to involve other school community members to welcome new students; students and teachers might craft a "Welcome to Our School Brochure"; more ambitious students might even create a DVD/virtual tour of the school. Create Student Buddies who take responsibility for helping new students become acquainted with the school, giving them a tour and introducing them to key personnel and other friendly students.

Classroom-Level Practices to Ease Transition

- Create a "New Student Box" that includes everything a new student might need (and might not be able to afford) such as notebooks, paper, pens and pencils, labels to affix to desks and lockers, etc. You might even include a trade book as a special "welcome to our class" gift.

- Prepare a "New Student File" with materials for parents— classroom and school rules, supply list, extra sets of supplies for those who can't afford them, copies of general parent letters, class schedule and special classes (art, music, library, P.E.), classroom rules and procedures, calendar of activities, activity ideas for home, things for the child to use at school (quick interest survey for the older child to complete), and any materials that help student and parents understand how your classroom works.

- Develop short assessments for reading, writing, and mathematics if records are delayed so you can quickly determine, without making the new student uncomfortable, what her needs and challenges might be.

- Introduce the student to the class and invite the student, to the extent she feels comfortable, to share information about herself.

- Introduce the student to other students who may have recently joined your class and who are succeeding. Find special time to speak one-to-one with the new student to make sure he understands and feels comfortable with everything there is to know; making time for friendly, informal conversation adds immeasurably to the student's comfort level.

- Monitor the student's academic transition—this is especially critical for new students who have already moved frequently. Arrange for a one-on-one tutor as needed or possible. Consider that the student may move again and laminate examples of best work to assure it's available for the next teacher if another move should occur. Consider also snapping photos of the child at work in your classroom and posing with new classmates so if he is forced to move again both he and his new teacher will have photos of his previous class.

When a Student Must Leave

- Invite classmates to write letters to their departing peer. If a student leaves without notice, the letters can be kept in the office file until records are requested and then sent to the student with the official record transfer.

- Prepare a "Goodbye Book." Invite students to share special comments and stories for their departing classmates. Include photographs of students and the classroom (consider creating a digital RealeBook that's easily assembled and shared).

- Prepare a departure file with sample work that the student can bring to the new school. Popp (2004) suggests including the following if possible: "exemplary work (laminate, if possible), journal recalling events from classmates, individual and class photos, self-addressed stamped envelopes to your school, stationery for the departing students to write back, a letter from the teacher introducing the student to his or her new teacher, trade books the student has read, and a note listing the similarities shared by schools to lessen anxiety of the unknown that children wonder about when starting in a new school."

- Explore the possibility of staying in touch by email and even corresponding with the student's new school and classmates.

School transfers and transitions are never easy but to the extent you and your school are able to anticipate and prepare for them, the highly mobile students you serve can count on a transition that's relatively easy and comfortable. Above all, your warmth and compassion will make the difference.

Developing a School/Classroom Demographic Profile

If family involvement is to become a reality in schools and classrooms rather than simply a professional dream, close attention must be paid to how the family has changed. Schools must also acknowledge that the cultural makeup of classrooms is changing in conjunction with the ethnic,

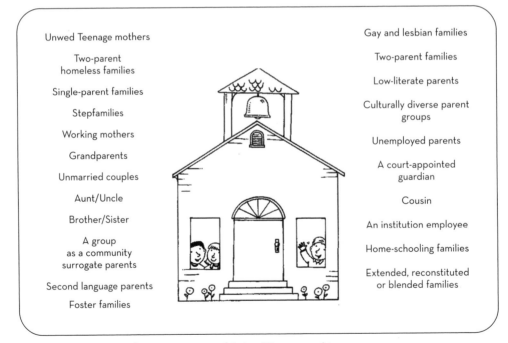

Figure 3.2: Pictorial Representation of School Demographics

cultural, and economic changes occurring in families in this country. (See Figure 3.2 for a pictorial description of the families with whom your school might have to open lines of communication.)

Demography is the study of a human population, its structure and change. The 2000 census data confirmed an increase in new majority "minority" populations. By 2020, children of color will constitute 46 percent of the public school population. Approximately 40 million people in the U.S. speak a maternal language that is not English. A Demographic School/Classroom Profile is a composite description of the parent community that exists in your school building, as well as in individual classrooms. The demographic profile data can be collected from the information on the student data cards, which are usually located in the principal's office.

The benefits of constructing a Demographic School/Classroom Profile are as follows:

- Allows teachers to develop tailor-made parentally appropriate activities

- Helps teachers to take a look at the history of parent involvement at the school level

- Allows teachers to determine whether parent involvement has been effective or not

- Gives teachers a way to pinpoint where problems may be occurring

- Allows teachers to interact with families in a way that is specific to their needs

- Provides teachers with an in-depth look at the strengths of a family/community

- Gives teachers real data and removes the guesswork/judgments/ assumptions about families

- Allows teachers to connect to families on a grade-by-grade basis

See Figure 3.3 to construct your school's demographic profile and Figure 3.4 to construct a classroom profile. (For additional information on school/classroom demographic profiles, see Edwards, 2004.)

Demographic School Profile

Use this chart to develop a demographic profile of your school. Enter in the number and percentage of students for each category. Include other categories that would be useful for your school.

		Number of Students	Percentage of Students
Sex	Male		
	Female		
Ethnicity	African American		
	Asian		
	Caucasian		
	Hispanic/Latino		
	Native American		
	Other		
Mother's Level of Education	Some High School		
	High School Graduate or Equivalent		
	Some College		
	College Graduate		
	Graduate/Professional Degree		
Father's Level of Education	Some High School		
	High School Graduate or Equivalent		
	Some College		
	College Graduate		
	Graduate/Professional Degree		
Employment	Mother Employed Full-time		
	Mother Employed Part-time		
	Mother Unemployed		
	Father Employed Full-time		
	Father Employed Part-time		
	Father Unemployed		
Lives With	Both Parents		
	Mother		
	Father		
	Other Guardian		
Languages Spoken at Home	English		
Form of Transportation	Bus		
	Walker		
	Drop-off		
	Other		
	Receives Free/Reduced Lunch		
	Frequency of Move In/Move Out		

Figure 3.3: Demographic School Profile

Demographic Classroom Profile

Name of Student	Age	Ethnicity	Lives With	Mother Education Level	Mother Occupation	Father Education Level	Father Occupation	Language Spoken at Home	Number of Siblings	Receives Free/Reduced Lunch	Distance Between Home and School	Bus, Walker, Drop-Off	Frequency of Move In/Move Out	Reading Level

Figure 3.4: Demographic Classroom Profile

Creating Homework Assignments That Make Sense

What can you learn from constructing school and classroom demographic profiles? For one thing, you can learn how many children are in a family and how you can better assign homework not as individual teachers, but as a staff. I have always felt that when teachers give homework assignments, they have to be mindful of the fact that when parents have more than one child and each child has homework on the same night, one if not all of the children might not receive help from the parents. Many parents work long hours, spend time doing long commutes, and when they come home and throw dinner on the table, there is very little time left to help with homework. Most of you will agree that coaches let parents know the schedule (i.e., time, dates, etc.) for the entire season. Unfortunately, few schools let parents know in August the dates they want them to help their child with homework throughout the school year. I am advocating that schools create a master schedule for homework assignments/activities. At the beginning of the school year, if each teacher critically examines the kind of assignments they have assigned throughout the year in the past, this information will be useful in helping them to complete the weekly homework assignment sheet and useful in developing the school-wide master homework schedule. For first-year teachers, I suggest that they meet with a mentor teacher to help them decide what homework activities they can assign throughout the year so that their activities can be incorporated into the school-wide master homework schedule. While this may seem impossibly ambitious and ultimately not possible, it's surely worth devoting at least one faculty meeting to a discussion of homework and developing a sense of each teacher's approach to homework. In this way, your school can reach an agreement about the kinds of homework it makes sense to assign and develop some general guidelines to assure it doesn't become too arduous. See Figures 3.5 and 3.6 to help you get started.

Homework Sheet

Teacher: _____ Week of: _____

Monday   Math:
               Word Study:
               Science:
               Social Studies:
               Language Arts:

Tuesday   Math:
               Word Study:
               Science:
               Social Studies:
               Language Arts:

Wednesday Math:
               Word Study:
               Science:
               Social Studies:
               Language Arts:

Thursday   Math:
               Word Study:
               Science:
               Social Studies:
               Language Arts:

Friday   Math:
               Word Study:
               Science:
               Social Studies:
               Language Arts:

Notes

Parent Signature: _____

Student Signature: _____

Figure 3.5: Classroom Homework Sheet

Schoolwide Homework Schedule

Example of a School Homework Schedule: Shaded days indicate when homework is to be assigned in that grade.

Grade Level	Monday	Tuesday	Wednesday	Thursday	Friday
First	▓		▓		
Second		▓		▓	
Third	▓		▓	▓	
Fourth	▓	▓		▓	
Fifth	▓	▓	▓	▓	

Figure 3.6: Schoolwide Homework Schedule

Next Steps

If a group of grade-level teachers are aware that they share multiple students from one family, such teachers can work together to plan homework assignments or projects that are interrelated. Alternatively, teachers could plan homework and projects designed so that older students could aid their younger siblings. Assigning homework and projects across grade levels that center around similar topics, tasks, or issues can also allow the parents to more fully engage in helping multiple children with assignments. Some of you might be aware of the arguments against assigning homework (Kohn, 2006; Bennet & Kalish, 2006), but others including Marzano & Pickering (2007) warn if a district or school discards homework completely, it will be throwing away a powerful instructional tool.

Chapter 4

Soliciting Helpful Information From Parents

Building school expectations based on the information you received from parents is another essential step in your journey for improving parent involvement at your school. I have included several strategies to put you on the right path. Parents, of course, vary widely in their available resources and background knowledge so, in the same way that we provide differentiated instruction for our students, we'll want to consider how we can best support parents. Flexibility and sensitivity are the dual keys to working effectively with parents.

To help you connect with your students' parents, I will introduce the following strategies:

- Defining *differentiated parenting* and *parentally appropriate*
- Determining parent capability, willingness, and responsibility
- Eliciting parent stories
- Finding out parents' views of their children
- Describing alternatives to home visits

- Outlining additional strategies for developing professional relationships with parents

Differentiated Parenting and Parentally Appropriate

As educators, you know that parents are not all the same. They have their own strengths and weaknesses, complexities, problems, and questions, and we must work with them and see them as more than "just parents." In my work with families, I coined two terms: *differentiated parenting* and *parentally appropriate* (Edwards, 2004). I proposed the concept of *differentiated parenting* as a way to urge schools not to place all parents into one basket. When schools design programs for parents, one size does not fit all. I used the term *parentally appropriate* to stress the point that "because parents are different, tasks and activities must be compatible with their capabilities" (p. 83). This is not to say that parents' goals for their children vary greatly (they all want their children to succeed in school), but it's clear that their situations, perspectives, and abilities affect their capacity to support their children in particular ways. For example, asking parents to read to their children appears to be a simple request. But some parents never experienced proper modeling of how to read interactively with children. They might not know what materials are most appropriate for children to read. They may also underestimate the positive effects of talking with their children about what the children have read. More than 15 years ago in my work with parents at Donaldsonville Elementary School in Louisiana, I learned from personal experience how uncomfortable parents felt when teachers asked them to read to their children. Such parents require different support than parents who might readily respond to the request to "read to your child" because of their own positive past experience.

The point I make is more subtle and significant than merely matching the school's request of parents with each parent's ability to respond. The greater point is that parents, like students, are best served when treated individually. This means knowing them, listening to their own stories, understanding what will be most helpful to them in raising their children and supporting their children's school learning. A parent's needs are not static; they change over time with the advancing age of their children. Parent programs require a scope and sequence and differentiation to meet the needs of the parent relative to the age and progress of the child. Has your school staff seriously considered the notion of differentiated parenting or parentally appropriate school involvement? If you have, my hat is off to you. If you haven't, I strongly suggest that you put this on your school's improvement list.

Determining Parent Capability, Willingness, and Responsibility

The simple request made by the teacher, "Read to your child," can be a nightmare to parents who cannot read themselves and it may evoke feelings of despair, inadequacy, frustration, and fear (Edwards, 1995). A good first step toward parentally appropriate school involvement is to determine what activities your parents feel capable of doing, are willing to do, and feel responsible for fulfilling. You can collect this information by using the surveys I developed (see Figures 4.1, 4.2, and 4.3) or you can develop your own instruments. The surveys that follow focus on family support for reading, but they can be tailored to assess other issues as well. For parents that you feel might not be able to complete the survey, you can personally interview them. If your school has a parent liaison, this might be something that they could do.

Parents can be involved in their child's reading program in several ways. Look at the activities below and tell how you feel about each activity. Circle the number of your answer.

Activities	Definitely Not Capable . . . Not Sure . . . Definitely Capable				
1. Reading to child	1	2	3	4	5
2. Helping child with words in stories	1	2	3	4	5
3. Listening to and talking about stories with my child	1	2	3	4	5
4. Talking about pictures modeling how to study in storybooks	1	2	3	4	5
5. Talking about the main idea in a story or book	1	2	3	4	5
6. Helping child write a story	1	2	3	4	5
7. Writing stories based on family experiences	1	2	3	4	5
8. Helping my child to identity words and in different places (e.g. on cereal boxes or in dictionaries)	1	2	3	4	5
9. Teaching about story characteristics (plot, theme, setting, characters)	1	2	3	4	5
10. Finding out about child's reading progress	1	2	3	4	5
11. Teaching child how to use resources (encyclopedias, dictionaries, almanacs, atlas)	1	2	3	4	5
12. Helping child with reading homework assignments	1	2	3	4	5
13. Providing books and magazines for the child to read	1	2	3	4	5
14. Showing a positive attitude toward reading	1	2	3	4	5
15. Providing experiences for child that are reading related (library trips or other activities that can be used to stimulate interest in reading)	1	2	3	4	5
16. Helping child learn what words mean	1	2	3	4	5
17. Controlling amount of television child watches	1	2	3	4	5
18. Working in the school as an aide, parent tutor, parent volunteer, assistant teacher, or other such jobs	1	2	3	4	5
19. Helping to reinforce what your child's teacher has taught	1	2	3	4	5
20. Setting standards for speech in the home	1	2	3	4	5

Of the activities above, which three do you think you would be *most capable* of doing as a parent? ___ ___ ___

Write the number of your answer on the blank line: ___ Activity I feel most capable of doing

___ Activity I feel second most capable of doing

___ Activity I feel third most capable of doing

Figure 4.1: Parental Involvement Capabilities

Some teachers assume all parents are willing to support their child's reading both at home and at school. How willing are you to participate in the following activities? Circle the number of your answer.

Activities	Definitely Not Willing	. . . Not Sure . . .			Definitely Willing
1. Attend workshops to help me understand my child's individual style of learning	1	2	3	4	5
2. Provide a quiet place for my child to rest, think, and work alone	1	2	3	4	5
3. Let child participate in community and school programs that offer rewards such as certificates or books	1	2	3	4	5
4. Control the amount of time my child spends watching TV and the types of programs	1	2	3	4	5
5. Read aloud to child every day	1	2	3	4	5
6. Attend PTA/PTO meetings and parent-teacher conferences regularly	1	2	3	4	5
7. Help child at home with reading assignments or other school work	1	2	3	4	5
8. Work in the school as an aide, parent tutor, parent volunteer, assistant teacher, or other such jobs	1	2	3	4	5
9. Broaden child's background of experiences, (take child on field trips and vacations, and to the public library or bookmobile)	1	2	3	4	5
10. Buy books and other educational materials for child to use at home	1	2	3	4	5
11. Find out child's reading progress	1	2	3	4	5
12. Attend parent reading workshop	1	2	3	4	5
13. Take a university course to prepare yourself to help child with reading assignments	1	2	3	4	5
14. Set standards for speech in the home that will enable my child to communicate easily outside the home	1	2	3	4	5
15. Provide children with a collection of books selected with their interests in mind	1	2	3	4	5
16. Provide my child with membership in Book Clubs	1	2	3	4	5
17. Subscribe to children's periodicals	1	2	3	4	5
18. Use reference books for example, dictionaries, encyclopedias, almanacs, etc.	1	2	3	4	5
19. Provide outside tutorial assistance for my child if necessary	1	2	3	4	5
20. Work to reinforce what the teacher has taught	1	2	3	4	5
21. Let my child read to me at home	1	2	3	4	5

Which three of these activities do you think you would be *most willing* doing as a parent? ___ ___ ___

Write the number of your answer on the blank line: ___ Activity I am most willing to do

___ Activity I am second most willing to do

___ Activity I am third most willing to do

Figure 4.2: Willingness to Participate in Child's Reading Program

Which of these activities do you feel parents should accept responsibility for in the school's reading program? Circle the number of your answer.

Activities	Definitely Not Responsible . . . Not Sure . . . Definitely Responsible				
1. Helping child with homework	1	2	3	4	5
2. Working in the school as an aide, parent tutor, parent volunteer, assistant teacher, or other such jobs	1	2	3	4	5
3. Arranging conferences with my child's teacher about reading progress	1	2	3	4	5
4. Going to workshops or other educational activities for parents at school	1	2	3	4	5
5. Taking part in PTA/PTO meetings	1	2	3	4	5
6. Helping children learn through the use of educational materials at home (games, magazines, books, newspapers)	1	2	3	4	5
7. Taking children to places with educational interest (museums, libraries, art galleries, etc.)	1	2	3	4	5
8. Controlling the amount of time child spends watching TV and the types of programs	1	2	3	4	5
9. Reading aloud to child every day	1	2	3	4	5
10. Letting child see me reading each day	1	2	3	4	5
11. Helping child add words to his/her speaking vocabulary	1	2	3	4	5
12. Setting standards for speech in the home that will enable child to communicate easily outside the home	1	2	3	4	5
13. Encouraging conversation in the home	1	2	3	4	5
14. Providing child with a collection of books selected with his/her interests in mind	1	2	3	4	5
15. Writing stories based on family experiences	1	2	3	4	5
16. Monitoring child's reading progress	1	2	3	4	5
17. Encouraging child to read every day	1	2	3	4	5
18. Encouraging child to write every day	1	2	3	4	5
19. Working to reinforce what the teacher has taught	1	2	3	4	5
20. Letting my child read to me at home	1	2	3	4	5
21. Helping child with reference books, i.e., dictionaries, encyclopedias, almanacs, atlas, etc.	1	2	3	4	5

Which three of these activities do you think you would be *most responsible* for carrying out as a parent? ___ ___ ___

Write the number of your answer on the blank line: ___ Activity I feel most responsible to do

___ Activity I feel second most responsible to do

___ Activity I feel third most responsible to do

Figure 4.3: Parent Responsibilities for Reading Instruction

Eliciting Parent Stories

Does your school ask parents about their literacy interactions with their children? If not, I suggest that you begin to do so. The way your school can get evidence of literacy interactions is to collect what I call "parent stories" of children's literacy development. This has been a very successful strategy for getting critical insights into the literacy interaction in a child's home environment from the parent's perspective. Based on what the parent shares, teachers are better able to determine if a child is entering a grade as an *emergent, early,* or *fluent* reader. Such stories also reflect other critical interactions between parents and children. For more information on how to collect parent stories, see *A Path to Follow: Learning to Listen to Parents* by Patricia A. Edwards, Heather M. Pleasants, and Heather Edwards.

According to Vandergrift & Greene (1992), "every parent has his or her own story to tell" (p. 57). Coles (1989) further contends that "one's response to a story is just as revealing as the story itself" (p. 18). In my work with Pleasants & Franklin (1999), we define "parent stories" as the narratives gained from open-ended conversations and/or interviews. In these interviews, parents respond to questions designed to provide information about traditional and nontraditional early literacy activities and experiences that have happened in the home. They also define parent stories through their ability to construct home literacy environments for teachers, and by their ability to connect home and school. By using stories as a way to express the nature of the home environment, parents can select anecdotes and personal observations from their own individual consciousnesses to give teachers access to complicated social, emotional, and educational issues that can help to unravel for teachers the mystery around their students' literacy beginnings. Some examples of the questions we used to collect parent stories are as follows:

- What do you and your child enjoy doing together?

- All children have potential. Did you notice that _____ had some particular talent or "gift" early on? If so, what was it? What did your child do to make you think that he or she had this potential?

Were there specific things you did as a parent to strengthen this talent? If so, what?

- Is there something about your child that might not be obvious to the teacher, but might positively or negatively affect his or her performance in school if the teacher knew?

- What activities or hobbies do you participate in as an individual? with your spouse or friends? as a family?

- Can you describe "something" about your home learning environment that you would like the school to build upon because you feel that this "something" would enhance your child's learning potential at school?

By using stories as a way to express the nature of the home environment, parents can select anecdotes and personal observations from their own individual consciousness to give teachers access to complicated social, emotional, and educational issues that can help to unravel for teachers the mysteries around their students' early literacy. Still further, we pointed out that many parents have vivid memories about the following:

- The kinds of routines they did with their children.

- Specific interactions they had with their children; observations of their children's beginning learning efforts.

- Ways in which their children learned simply by watching them.

- Perceptions as to whether their occupation determined how they raised their children.

- Descriptions of "teachable moments" they had with their children.

- Descriptions of things about their children that may not be obvious to the teacher but would help their children's performance if the teacher knew about them.

Additionally, many parents have scrapbooks, audiocassettes, videotapes, DVDs, photographs, or other artifacts to share that provide insight into their children's literacy histories.

Parent stories can provide teachers with the opportunity to gain a deeper understanding of the "human side" of families and children (e.g., children's behavior, children's ways of learning and communicating, problems parents have encountered and ways in which these problems may have impacted their children's views about school and the schooling process). On a final note, we suggest that because teachers' evaluations of students are sometimes based on quick observations, they frequently fail to take into account the experiences that students have brought with them to school. Teachers are thus lacking vital information which can help them better understand and teach their students. Parents can fill in some of the missing pieces by providing stories about their child's early learning experiences at home.

Finding Out Parents' Views of Their Children

A parent letter is another strategy to get the parents' perspective on their children. Parents who might feel uncomfortable writing a letter might tape record their thoughts about their child. You might consider creating a template for your parents to make it easier for them to write a letter to you; for example, parents might include something about:

- their family—ages of other siblings
- their child's previous schooling experience
- extracurricular activities their child enjoys
- concerns you or their child has

I have included a sample letter on the following page written by a very sophisticated parent as a demonstration of the sort information a parent might include.

Alternatives to Home Visits

For years, some early childhood teachers have made the argument for home visits. The term "home visit" as related to childcare programs has several interpretations. A home visit may occur when a teacher or caregiver visits the home of an enrolled child to observe that child and to

Sample parent letter

Dear Mrs. Emmons,

First, let me tell you we are thrilled that our son, Nikolas, has been chosen to be in your class and in the looping program! I believe your background and the consistency of looping will give Nikolas the stimulation and stability he so desperately needs.

Let me introduce you to Nikolas:

Nikolas started at Discovery in Mrs. Hughes' DK—something I believe was a true gift to all of us. He has a late birthday (Oct. 5), and that extra year helped him develop the social skills and maturity necessary to succeed in Mrs. Graves' kindergarten last year.

He is an incredibly bright boy—and that is sometimes a source of difficulty for him and his teachers. He struggles to find peers with whom he can relate. While he has friends, we are eager for him to find a real buddy—or two! As an only child at home, Nikolas is usually surrounded by adults and older neighborhood children. He craves a peer group that he can hang out with.

That said, he typically gets along well with children at school and at childcare—which he will no longer attend this year. Nikolas started school as a pretty aggressive, bossy child, and that continues, though he is learning what is and isn't appropriate in that realm. He will likely try to be your co-disciplinarian, alerting you to the misbehavior of others, but often dodging responsibility for his own misdeeds.

Nikolas is extremely hard on himself, and I suspect that some of that is internal and some of that stems from our high standards for him. We have backed off pressuring him to perform as we have seen it backfire. So we try to support, encourage, and praise! At the same time, we do not want to reward him when the job is not done well! Our hope is that Nikolas will continue learning to cope with and learn from his mistakes. He tends not to volunteer much in class—perhaps out of fear of failure. And he struggles to try new things and new approaches to old things—again we think this is because he does not want to do something until he

(continued . . .)

(continued . . .)

is certain he will do it perfectly. His holding back does, however, pay off, as he usually gets it right when he finally decides to go for it!

Nikolas once told me, "Mom, I'd rather exercise my mind than my body, so stop trying to get me into sports!" That all changed when he discovered gymnastics last winter! Nikolas is quite a performer in the Twistars gymnastics program—one of his extracurriculars.

We believe in the balanced approach to life outside of school. Nikolas can do one sport and one academic (or other) extracurricular per season. He loves science, art, and inventing, and we expect to enroll him in something related to one of those areas in addition to his gymnastics this fall.

We value family time above all else and strive to spend at least a couple of hours every night interacting with Nikolas. We talk about school, current events (we watch the news and talk about it with him), hopes, dreams, and how much we love one another. As much as possible, we spend our weekends at our cottage in Higgins Lake, where we have uninterrupted, quality family time.

Nikolas has two dogs, one an aging yellow lab and the other a brand new standard poodle puppy. If anything motivates him, it is his love of dogs and his passion for monsters. Since learning to read last year, Nikolas has devoured monster books. He is currently obsessed with the adolescent series Goosebumps by R.L. Stine—the boy *actually* is reading those books on his own. I do not believe there is anything we as parents can do that is better than reading to our boy—we have missed fewer than ten days of reading to him since the day we brought him home from the hospital.

We know we will get to know you well over the coming two years, and we look forward to it. We are passionate advocates for public education and for our child. Professionally, I am the Director of Communications for the MEA and Nikolas' dad is a professional photographer. You can count on us to support you and our child throughout the coming year.

Best wishes!!

Margaret and Daymon Hartley

talk to the parents or guardians in the home environment. A visit also may be indicated if a child is absent for several days due to sickness or other reasons, or to provide services to the family. The term "home visit" may also mean a visit by a resource person or monitoring personnel to the home of a family childcare provider. This visit allows the caregiver to better understand the child's unique strengths and needs, and provides an opportunity for parents and staff to discuss childcare and early education issues. Some parents may be intimidated or uncomfortable talking with staff in the childcare setting, so these informal gatherings in the home may empower parents and facilitate more discussion.

Many teachers at your school may feel uncomfortable visiting the homes of their students for a variety of reasons (e.g., violent/unsafe neighborhood, etc.). It has been well documented that parents are their children's first teachers. If your school is able to supply families with disposable cameras, parents will be able to share insights that your school staff might not observe on a one-time home visit. Allowing parents to discuss and share these pictures with you is an excellent mechanism for understanding a child's literacy environment and for getting to know the families. This strategy can also be used in the upper grades.

I know that some of you are scratching your heads and saying, I don't know whether I want to give up on the idea of home visits. If you feel comfortable doing home visits, I encourage you to continue. However, I still strongly encourage you to purchase disposable cameras for parents. Perhaps, the combination of doing a home visit and having parents share pictures with you depicting their home literacy environment is a win-win situation for your school and the families and children you serve.

Strategies for Developing Professional Relationships With Parents

Increasingly, schools are discovering it's wise not to take anything for granted. Accordingly, they are writing out their expectations for parents and sharing them with the parents in the form of contracts. Ideally, parents and teachers read and sign the contract side-by-side so both parties understand what's expected and agree to meet the expectations in order to provide the best education possible for the child.

Parenting Contracts

Parenting contracts are a new and supportive provision and will enable formal agreements between parent and school in which each side sets out the steps they will take to secure an improvement in the child's literacy development, attendance, and behavior. Some parents seek such help themselves, but others need a more directive approach, and a parent contract is a concrete strategy for accomplishing this. An example of a parenting contract follows on pages 70–71.

Classroom Contracts

Your school should also have classroom contracts that are signed by the parent and the student. This contract serves as a wake-up call to students. First, the contract should be posted in each classroom at all times. Second, the teacher explains in detail to students and parents the classroom contract and what happens when the contract is broken: (1) students will be given a warning when they break the contract, (2) the student will be told what part of the contract he or she broke and when, (3) the teacher will ask the child's parent to discuss the contract, and (4) the student must complete the assignment and turn it in the next day. Please keep in mind that a wake-up call is simply a reminder that a change is needed.

Developing a Scope and Sequence of Parent Involvement

Over 20 years ago, Carol Seefeldt (1985) stated that schools should communicate with parents through the curriculum. She correctly noted that educators should do the following:

> Capitalize on the curriculum as a means of communicating with parents. It is an ongoing way to keep parents totally informed of their child's day, the school's goals and objectives, and the meaning of early childhood education. It's one way to begin to establish close, meaningful communication with busy parents. Remember— informed, involved parents, those who are aware of what their children do in an early childhood program, are also supportive parents (p. 25).

I agree with Seefeldt. I coined the term Scope and Sequence of Parent Involvement, which I defined as grade-level family involvement activities that are built around the elementary school literacy curriculum (Edwards, 2004, p. 283). I firmly believe that teachers and the whole school "family" have the responsibility for encouraging and facilitating parents' exposure to and integration into their children's classroom curriculum. I also believe that families and children must learn the culture of the school while they are attempting to master academic tasks.

In constructing a scope and sequence, your school needs to have a clear plan and a set of goals that you would like to achieve at each grade level and decide how parents can assist with this plan or set of goals. This strategy provides the opportunity for the school staff to try their own hand at developing a scope and sequence of parent involvement on a grade-by-grade basis. In my work with families who participated in the four-year home literacy project, I observed the following (see Edwards, 2004, pp. 211–212):

> Some parents joined in to affirm their children's growth and to describe their children's writing initiatives at home, whereas others raised concerns about their children's reticence and lack of initiative. Teachers shared their work, plans, questions, and uncertainties about differences in students' development as writers.

The parent meetings established a predictable structure for parents to communicate information about how their child was responding to instruction in school. Parents not only became more knowledgeable about the school curriculum, but they also contributed information about their children's struggles, concerns, and progress. They began to inform other parents and teachers about their children's desires, and they made sense of the topics, audiences, and kernel issues in children's lives. Many parents gave each other ideas about how they wrote with their children and what ideas had stirred their children's curiosity.

Parents became more than recipients and overseers of assignments. Their creative responses also changed the dynamics of the informant group. There was a mutual sense of pride and enjoyment, shared by parents and professional educators alike, in reading the children's writing and explaining

Sample parenting contract

Pupil's Name: _____

Parents' Names: _____

Teacher's Name and Name of School: _____

Teacher's Contact Details: _____

Background to Parenting Contract

Following a meeting on April 14th between Mr. Perry (the student's teacher), Mr. & Mrs. Taylor (the student's parents), and Todd (the student), we have all agreed that we want to work together to help Todd. [*Here we indicate what exactly we want Todd to improve in regard to literacy achievement, attendance, behavior, and so on.*]

What has been agreed?

The School's Promise

Mrs. Jones has agreed to help Todd's parents help Todd. [*Here the teacher list specifics for helping Todd to improve in regards to literacy achievement, attendance, or behavior.*]

- Send Todd's parents a behavior report at the end of every day so that they know if there have been any problems.

- Be available between 4 and 4:30 every day if there is anything that Mr. or Mrs. Taylor want to discuss in person.

Mr. & Mrs. Taylor's Promise

- Sign the copy of the behavior report and let Mrs. Jones know whether they have comments to make.

- Inform Mrs. Jones if they are encountering any problems with the homework assignments.

(continued . . .)

Review

Mrs. Jones, Mr. & Mrs. Taylor, and Todd will meet again [include the date] to discuss how things are going and whether this agreement needs to be changed in any way.

Important Dates/Useful Contact Details

Mrs. Jones: _____

Mrs. Rogers, Parenting Support Practitioner: _____

Mrs. Terry, Literacy Coach: _____

If Mrs. Rogers and Mrs. Terry are unavailable contact: _____

_____

Mr. Terry, Principal: _____

Agreement

We will do what we have agreed on in this parenting contract and will work together to help Todd improve his literacy achievement, attendance, and/or behavior.

Signed:

Mrs. Jones _____

Date: _____

Mr. Taylor _____

Date: _____

Mrs. Taylor _____

Date: _____

Classroom Contract

I, _____ understand the
importance of having and following rules in school. I agree that the rules listed below are
fair and will help make Room 114 a better place to learn. I agree to follow the rules listed
below from now until the end of the second-grade year. I understand that if I break the
rules, Miss Johnson will discuss with me the consequences she feels are necessary.

ROOM 114 RULES

1. I will respect others' bodies, feelings, and property.

2. I will keep my hands, feet, and objects to myself.

3. I will walk quietly in the hall.

4. I will listen when others are speaking.

5. I will follow directions the first time they are given.

6. I will come to school prepared to learn.

7. I will have books, papers, pencils, and homework ready for class.

Student signature _____

Date _____

Parent signature _____

Date _____

Figure 4.4: Classroom Contract

life situations and humorous events such as how a garage sale treasure (a plastic fruit-covered hat) became a critical component in a story. They also shared a mutual frustration over students who refused to write or share their work with their classmates. Rather than just expediting the meetings, teachers reaped rewards by openly sharing their struggles, as well as hearing from parents about the positive effects of their teaching. For example, one parent publicly praised the work of his child's teacher and described his responses to a relative who criticized the public schools within the district. Other parents described their child's excitement about writing with friends as a sleepover activity. Parents received support from the school and also from other parents.

Next Steps

- Ask parents to complete the Parent Capability, Willingness, and Responsibility Survey. This information will prove informative.

- Parent accountability is important. Parenting and classroom contracts can help you succeed with a wide range of families.

Chapter 5

Getting More Parents Involved

Parent communication and recruitment is the final step in your journey for moving parent involvement from high rhetoric to high practice. Many of you have probably had breakfast meetings, Saturday morning sessions, back-to-school nights, picnics, workshops, carnivals, fairs, suppers, and even established a phone tree to communicate with and recruit families. In an effort to improve home-school relationships at your school, some of you have prepared parent-information packets, created monthly or annual calendars highlighting upcoming school events and meetings, provided home-school handbooks, sent happy-grams, August letters, spontaneous notes, weekly newsletter updates for parents, as well as developed a web page, but you still feel that you are not reaching the families you need to reach. I have included several strategies to help broaden your thinking about parent communication and recruitment.

Parent Communication and Recruitment

- Tapping the social world of the parent
- Soliciting the help of community leaders
- Constructing a profile of the forms of home/school contacts
  —Communication checklist as worksheet to help school staffs evaluate the notification, preparation, content, and quality of face-to-face communication with parents

—Communication checklist to evaluate the frequency, quality, content, and distribution of the school's written communication

—Parent communication log

—Categories of letters/information sent to parents

- Categories of Multimedia for Increased Parent Communication

—Develop a web page

—Send weekly email updates for parents

—Establish a homework "hotline" or "video homework hotline" for parents to use to check and view homework assignments

Earlier, I asked the question, "Do you feel frustrated when parents do not return notes or answer phone calls and fail to check their child's homework?" I am sure that some of you said to yourself, "Yes, we have parents like that in our school." The label we use to characterize these parents is "hard-to-reach." However, Taylor & Dorsey-Gaines (1988) believe:

> If we are to teach, we must first examine our own assumptions about families and children, and we must be alert to the negative images in the literature . . . Instead of responding to pathologies, we must recognize that what we see may actually be healthy adaptations to an uncertain and stressful world. As teachers, researchers, [administrators], and policy-makers, we need to think about the children themselves and try to imagine the contextual worlds of their day-to-day lives. (p. 203)

Some of you may be working with parents who are having a difficult time moving successfully through Maslow's Hierarchy of Needs. This is a theory in psychology that Abraham Maslow proposed in his 1943 paper *A Theory of Human Motivation,* which he subsequently extended to include his observations of humans' innate curiosity. Maslow's theory contended that as humans meet basic needs, they seek to satisfy successfully higher needs that occupy a set hierarchy. Maslow's hierarchy of needs is often depicted as a pyramid consisting of five levels: the four lower levels are grouped together as deficiency needs associated with physiological needs, while the top level is termed growth needs and is what drives personal growth. The higher needs in this hierarchy only come into focus once all of the lower needs in the pyramid are satisfied. Once an individual has moved past a level, those needs will no longer be prioritized. However, if a lower set of needs is no longer being met, the individual will temporarily reprioritize those needs—dropping down to that level until the lower needs are reasonably satisfied again.

Renee White-Clark and Larry Decker (1996) examined Maslow's Hierarchy of Needs and parent involvement in terms of parent concerns and staff support. A summary of their findings is on the following page.

As teachers, you must face up to your own misconceptions about "hard-to-reach" parents. Davies (1988) contends that these flawed perceptions may include:

- Regarding poor families as deficient, seeing only their problems and not their strengths

- Believing that the problems of "hard-to-reach" families are the fault of the families themselves

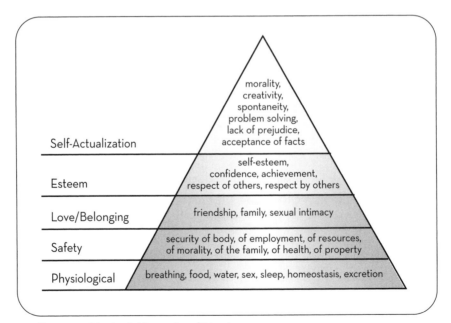

Figure 5.1: Maslow's Hierarchy of Needs

Self-Fulfillment Needs (*ego fulfillment*)	**Parent Concerns** • Can I really accomplish my goals? • What is my potential as a person, parent, mate, breadwinner, etc.? • Will I be able to acquire new skills or enhance present skills?	**Staff Support** • Highlight parents' contributions to the program • Assess skills and potential • Develop interest areas • Plan for upward mobility • Facilitate goal identification
Esteem Needs (*"I am lovable and capable."*)	**Parent Concerns** • Am I doing something worthwhile?	**Staff Support** • Will I be looked up to? • Will I learn a new skill or gain new knowledge? • Provide successful experiences • Give positive feedback • Encourage decision making • Encourage volunteering
Social Needs (*family, friends, groups*)	**Parent Concerns** • Will I be able to make friends? • Will I be accepted by others? • Should I belong to a group? • Do others really need me?	**Staff Support** • Develop parent/staff partnerships • Help arrange social events • Support parent/child activities • Identify recreation facilities • Encourage buddy system
Safety Needs (*job, home, security*)	**Parent Concerns** • Will I be able to get a job? • Will I get a "fair break"? • Will I find something to hold onto? • Will I feel safe and comfortable?	**Staff Support** • Identify community resources • Make referrals • Provide counseling • Encourage independence
Physiological Needs (*food, clothing, shelter*)	**Parent Concerns** • Will I be able to provide adequate clothing for the family? • Will I be able to locate housing? • Will I be able to provide a balanced diet?	**Staff Support** • Provide emergency information • Establish crisis intervention procedures • Provide information about resources in the community

I suggest that your school must be willing to experiment with new approaches to home-school-community interactions and be willing to restructure in ways that address families' needs for flexible time frames, childcare, and transportation. Atkin, Bastiani, & Goode (1988) suggested that:

> Schools seeking to improve their relationship with parents and to create conditions for better communication [should know that] different parents value different forms of contact! The hard fact is that parents are not a homogenous body any more than teachers are. They have their own individual ways of making judgments about schools, their preferred ways of seeking and receiving information, their own standpoints on the extent to which they wish to be involved with their child's education. The implications of this are that schools need to plan a range and variety of forms of contact in the knowledge that no one particular type will suit all parents (p. 128).

I couldn't agree more with Atkin, Bastiani, & Goode's observation and I am sure you do as well. You probably use letters as the bread and butter of communication between home and school, and letters are probably the most frequent form of contact that your school has with your parents. There are four categories of letters in Figure 5.2 (giving information, transfer, general matters, and seeking information).

I suggest that your school make every effort to translate all of your written communication into the different languages spoken in your students' homes. It is also important that your school do an analysis of whether your best form of contact is through the written or spoken word.

Your school staff can use a verbal teacher-parent communication checklist to help you evaluate the notification, preparation, content, and quality of face-to-face communication with parents.

Your school staff can also use a written teacher-parent communication checklist to help you evaluate the frequency, quality, content, and distribution of the school's written communication.

By now, I hope you have completed a School and Classroom Demographic Profile so you know the types of families who attend your school. This information should help you with your analysis.

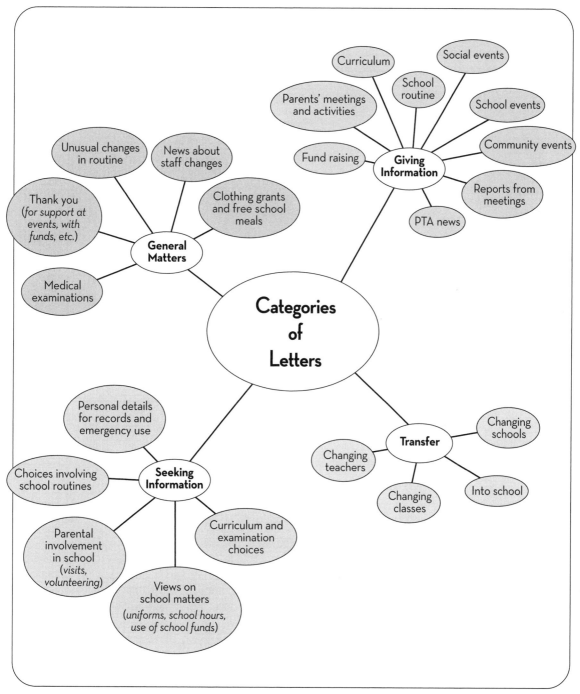

Figure 5.2: Categories of Letters

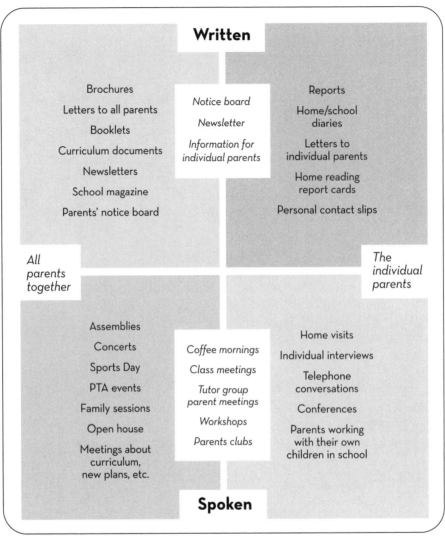

Written

Brochures

Letters to all parents

Booklets

Curriculum documents

Newsletters

School magazine

Parents' notice board

Notice board

Newsletter

Information for individual parents

Reports

Home/school diaries

Letters to individual parents

Home reading report cards

Personal contact slips

All parents together

The individual parents

Assemblies

Concerts

Sports Day

PTA events

Family sessions

Open house

Meetings about curriculum, new plans, etc.

Coffee mornings

Class meetings

Tutor group parent meetings

Workshops

Parents clubs

Home visits

Individual interviews

Telephone conversations

Conferences

Parents working with their own children in school

Spoken

Figure 5.3: Profile of the Forms of Home/School Contacts

Although schools and teachers rely heavily on traditional forms of written and verbal communication (e.g., monthly newsletter, phone call home, note to parents), there are many other ways that can be used to inform parents about the school, the classroom, events, and expectations.

Verbal Teacher-Parent Communication

Directions: Use this worksheet to evaluate the notification, preparation, content, and quality of your face-to-face or other verbal communications with parents. In each square (when applicable) put a "+" for above average, a "o" for average, or a "-" for below average. This quick check will help you see your strengths as well as the areas in need of improvement. Add other communications not listed or criteria you feel are important.

Face-to-Face Verbal Communication	Early Publicity	Multiple Methods of Notification	Adequate Preparation	Clear Purpose for Meetings or Contact	Clear Agenda or Questions to Aid Preparation	Childcare Available	Translators Available if Required	Helpful to Parents	Focus on Child	Attendance Goal Met
Classroom Orientation										
Back-to-School Nights										
Open Houses										
Parent Education Meetings										
Parent-Teacher Conferences										
Telephone Conversations										
Coffee Meetings										
Home Visits										
Class or School Breakfasts										
Special Events										
Presentation to Community Groups										

Figure 5.4: Verbal Teacher-Parent Communication

Written Teacher-Parent Communication

Directions: Use this worksheet to evaluate the frequency, quality, content, and distribution of your school's written communications with parents. In each square (when applicable) put a " + " for above average, a "O" for average, or a " – " for below average. This quick check will help you see your strengths as well as the areas in need of improvement. Add other communications not listed or criteria you feel are important.

Written Communication	Frequent	Easy to Read	Neat and Attractive	Encourages and Allows for Responses	Focuses on Important Information	Focus on Academics	Timely Distribution	Distributed to All Involved	Translations Available
Classroom Policies									
Class Newsletters									
Progress Notes									
Success Reports									
Late/Missing Homework									
Excessive Tardies/Absences									
Incomplete Classwork									
Explanations of Assignments									
Assignment of Activities Calendar									
Course Requirements									
Learning Objectives									
Meeting Notices									
School Newsletters									
Handbooks									
School Policies discipline code, homework policy, health regulations, absences/tardies									
Parent Surveys									

Figure 5.5: Written Teacher-Parent Communication

Make Videos for Parents

No matter what you do, there will always be parents who fail to attend after-school literacy activities, visit your classroom, attend parent/teacher conferences, or read newsletters. Use technology to your advantage! Talk to your principal about creating a video to advertise your school to the community. Include such things as a tour of the building, behavioral expectations for students, staff and student interviews, learning goals, points of pride, and so forth. Reach out for funding. Go to the local newspaper and news channel to generate support from the community. You may also want to tape yourself explaining your current literacy program. What are my goals? Why is literacy so important? What do parents need to do in order for their children to succeed? Copy your program onto a DVD and send it home with students. We live in a technological society where people watch videos rather than read books. Since this is now a reality, schools could encourage teachers to develop videos of specific lessons, introducing families to what they can expect throughout the year.

Develop a Web Page

Creating a classroom web page will allow parents easy access to what's happening in your class. You can include up-to-date assignments and projects, current events, future projects, test dates, or any reminders that are worth mentioning. If you are not tech-savvy and have difficulty creating a web page, you can give parents your email address so that they can send you messages. Of course, you will need to check your email every night during the school week and respond appropriately and in a timely manner. You can also create an email discussion list (Yahoogroups and Google Groups both provide free web space for such groups) so that you can send messages to parents.

Weekly Email Updates for Parents

By making a mailing list with all of their parents' email addresses, teachers can help parents stay involved with events and curriculum topics covered weekly in their class. The email could cover help-session times for the week, current curriculum topics, dates of quizzes and tests for the week, lists of fun activities completed in class, and also could include live Internet links that would allow parents to print worksheets and help their child at home. Parents without an email address should get a print-out of the email sent home.

Something to Consider . . .

Developing a web page and weekly email updates for parents is great, but some families don't have computers. Children from disadvantaged backgrounds are at risk of falling behind at school and in the workforce due to poor access to technology. I don't have to convince you that having access to computers and the Internet is critical to ensuring a young person's success at school. The ability to access the Internet has become increasingly important to immerse oneself in the economic, political, and social aspects of the United States and the world. The idea of the "digital divide" refers to the growing gap between the underprivileged members of society, especially poor, rural, elderly, and handicapped portions of the population who do not have access to computers or the Internet; and the wealthy, the middle-class, and the young Americans living in urban and suburban areas who do have access.

I suggest that you develop home, school, and community partnerships to help those families who do not have a home computer. For example, your school can partner with churches, libraries, malls, Boys and Girls Clubs, to name a few, and help provide broader access to computers.

Create a Homework Hotline

This is not necessarily a new idea, but one that I think would be useful for schools to develop. The term *homework hotline* is often used to refer not only to those systems that provide live tutoring for assignments, but also automated services providing feedback and information regarding assignments. For instance, the latter type might allow a parent or student who is unaware of the current assignment to dial a number to connect to a prerecorded message from a specific teacher that describes the daily assignment. The automated system may also provide other school or classroom news. The content of an automated system may be either general (i.e., directed toward an entire school and/or classroom) or specific to the individual student. If student-specific, it might consist of individually recorded messages that provide information for the parents on whether their child's previous assignment had been completed, what the current assignment is, and an additional phone number for help or clarification (Garner, 1991). In contrast with live tutoring hotlines, these automated systems are generally available 24 hours a day (Glazer & Williams, 2001).

Other mechanisms for providing homework help include (a) answering machine systems that allow students to call, leave a number, and have their call returned, when convenient, by the tutor; (b) Internet resources (e.g., chat rooms, bulletin boards, email, blogs, wikis, etc.) that allow students to present questions and receive answers; and (c) educational television programming that incorporates on-air calls (Sang, 1986). I would like to add a fourth mechanism—homework videos. Over time, schools might develop simple videos that demonstrate key concepts that parents can check out and use to help their child. These might include everything from how to tackle long division, a five-paragraph essay, or conduct original research using multiple sources. New technology tools like Apple's iMovie makes this relatively simple and inexpensive to do and some enterprising parent might enjoy creating a DVD homework archive that parents can check out as needed to help their child.

Soliciting the Help of Community Leaders

Sometimes asking community leaders to contact parents who have literacy problems will provide the incentive parents need to become willing participants in a literacy program. Another approach is to ask parents to contact other parents who would benefit from the program. Both of these grassroots methods can build strong ties between the home and school, which, if carefully nurtured, will improve over time.

Timing is very important when recruiting community leaders to participate in your program and to help you involve parents. Like a farmer who must plant seeds during a certain season to reap the benefits of a good crop, you must recruit community leaders early enough to reap full participation and commitment from them. Leaders should not be contacted as an afterthought. Rather, they should be recruited long before the program sessions begin. You will find that most people in power positions prefer to be at the forefront of change, throwing their support to winning teams that might bring them political gain. No one likes to be contacted late in the game when the very survival of a program might be in jeopardy.

Because community leaders often have ties to families that teachers and administrators do not have, "parents and leaders," according to Susan Swap (1987), "are more in need of each other's support than even before" (p. 1). Community leaders can help identify hard-to-reach parents and recruit them; devise alternative solutions to school problems and help implement them. Without a doubt, community leaders represent a powerful force that can support parents and teachers and help them to achieve their goals.

Forming a Community Network

Schools are burdened with immense problems that affect the quality of education and the relationship with families and the community. Unless educators begin to enlist the support and involvement of parents and community leaders to help resolve these problems, education and high-quality community resources remain in jeopardy. Forming a community network will make a difference. It will help people feel that they have a stake in the success of the program and in creating better human resources. The result will be a program that has long-lasting effects in the school community.

One of the criticisms of the programs designed for poor and minority parents is that they are based upon the perception that such families won't come to school because they are not interested in helping their children. In order to dispel this belief when implementing the *Parents as Partners* program (see Edwards, 1990), I asked for community support in recruiting parents for the book-reading program. A major component contributing to the success of the *Parents as Partners* program was the community. The principal and assistant helped in identifying key community leaders, such as the Ministerial Alliance, business leaders, school-board members, and the local superintendent. They also suggested holding a series of meetings at the community center to solicit support from the ordinary townspeople (e.g., grandmothers and bus drivers), and contacting people just sitting on street corners about the role they could play in recruiting parents for the book-reading program. Each of these strategies proved to be successful.

The community support of the *Parents as Partners* was overwhelming. Ministers, black and white, agreed to preach from their pulpits about the importance of helping children learn to read. They regularly urged parents to attend the weekly reading sessions to learn to help their children in school, noting the importance of literacy as a tool of faith.

A local bar owner emerged as a strong supporter of the reading program, informing parents who patronized his establishment that they would no longer be welcome unless they put as much time into learning how to read to their children as they spent enjoying themselves at his bar. He provided transportation to school and back home for participating mothers and secured funds from the city social-services department for childcare for parents who otherwise could not attend. A grandmother organized a campaign to telephone program participants each week and to remind them of the scheduled meetings. I visited beauty salons, mom-and-pop restaurants, and local grocery stores to ask for their assistance in spreading the word about the book-reading program to the families in the community. A bus driver offered to drive parents to the program each week. Lastly, the older, retired people sitting on the street corners began to talk about the program and encouraged all the parents they came in contact with to attend.

The outpouring of support from the community was duplicated at Donaldsonville Elementary School, where school administrators, teachers, and the librarians staunchly supported the book-reading program. The teachers, as well as the school administrators and the librarian, enrolled in a family literacy course I taught to broaden their knowledge of literacy development in different family structures. Teachers also assisted in the development of training materials designed to show parents effective book-reading behaviors. The principal and assistant principal helped to publicize the program in the community, driving parents to the program each week and creating a friendly and warm environment at the school for the parents. The librarian designed a computer program that listed the names of each child whose parent was participating in the book-reading program. For the first time in the school's history, parents were able to check out up to five books under their child's name. The librarian also kept a computerized list of books the parents were checking out. This information was shared with me, the child's teacher. More importantly, the teachers, school administrators, and the librarian began to accept the parents as useful and reliable resources.

Networking in a Large Metropolitan Area

After reading what we did to recruit parents in the Donaldsonville community, you may be saying to yourself, "I don't live in a small rural community; I live in a large city. I have been extremely unsuccessful in recruiting parents to school events. How can I recruit parents to participate in programs like the *Parents as Partners* program in the school in which I teach?"

If you live in a large metropolitan area, many of the families you serve do not live in the community where the school is located. This creates its own kind of problems: namely, how you will get parents from across town to buy into the program and attend the sessions; secondly, how you will become acquainted with the parents and the communities in which they live.

I would recommend that you request the services of a demographer to determine the size, distribution, and vital statistics of the population in a given area. A demographer will provide valuable information about the families you serve and the significant contacts you should make.

However, if your school or school district is unable to utilize the services of a demographer, you might contact some of the following organizations within the community where your parents live. They will provide information about families and the social pressures parents encounter. They might even offer suggestions as to how you can effectively recruit for the program.

- Social Services Department

- Urban League

- Drug rehabilitation services

- Big Brothers/Big Sisters

- Shelters for abused women

- Law enforcement services

- Health Department services

- Alcoholics Anonymous

- City council

In addition, you can obtain a map of the area(s) in which the students and their parents live and circle businesses, organizations, churches, and other community support groups that can help you to identify and recruit community leaders. Have volunteers contact these sources by phone or letter, introduce the program to them, and invite them to a meeting.

The Social World of the Parent

As you examine your community to identify its leaders, look beyond the highly visible and articulate personalities of the dominant culture. Within every subculture, there are powerful leaders who directly influence their communities. The suggestions we have offered here for identifying and recruiting community leaders are based on a model developed by Bronfenbrenner, Cochran, & Cross at Cornell University (see Figure 5.6).

This model identifies the people and environmental forces that affect a person. The inner circle represents a person's immediate family, usually people who live in the household. Each larger circle, radiating from the middle represents a less immediate force. The next larger circle represents the individual's informal network—people who influence him or her directly, either positively or negatively. Relatives and friends are part of this network, but it might also include teachers or religious leaders with whom the individual has a personal relationship. The third circle represents institutions, agencies, or organizations that affect the person, sometimes only indirectly. The largest circle includes the societal values and norms that affect individuals.

The Social World of the Parent

Social Values and Norms

Institutions, Agencies, Organizations
Which include people such as

- Director of Adult Basic Education Programs
- Teen parent programs such as Parents Too Soon
- Social Service department
- Housing authority
- Health department
- Fraternal organizations
- PTA or PTO groups
- Lions Club/Jaycees/Rotary/Kiwanis
- Chamber of Commerce

Informal Network
Which include people such as

- Religious leaders/ministerial alliance/ circle groups at church
- Grandparents/aunts/uncles
- Small neighborhood business owners
- Teachers (retired and otherwise)
- Big Buddy, Big Brother, Big Sister organizations

Immediate Family

Figure 5.6: Identifying and Recruiting Community Leaders

What each of the illustrations or strategies in this section has in common is a purposeful effort to use the parents and familial culture and experiences to support children's academic performance. In summary, you need to:

- Create academic tasks that build on, extend, or develop areas of parental expertise, interests, or needs.

- Draw from institutional and classroom interaction norms that acknowledge the cultural patterns from which children emerge and the resources they have available.

- Develop relationships where power and responsibility are shared between parents and teachers.

These suggestions are all based on the assumption that both teachers and parents are of central importance to the academic success of students and equally critical in the development of school-based literacy expertise.

Closing Comments

The specific journey of writing this book is over, but the journey of working with parents does not end. I don't believe that my book provides an endpoint or a complete solution to the problems inherent in bridging the gap between teachers, schools, and communities—but I believe, and I hope you agree with me, that it gets us closer. My challenge to you is to begin to use the strategies and to pass the word on to other educators. Working together, we can build home/school partnerships that assure our students the most effective, supportive education possible.

References

Ascher, C. (1988). Improving the school-home connection for poor and minority urban students. *The Urban Review, 20*(2), 109–123.

Atkin, J., Bastiani, J., & Goode, J. (1988). *Listening to parents: An approach to the improvement of home-school relations.* New York: Croom Helm.

Bennett, S., & Kalish, N. (2006). *The case against homework: How homework is hurting our children and what we can do about it.* New York: Crown.

Cochran, M., Larner, M., Riley, D., Gunnarson, L., & Henderson, C. (1990). *Extending families: The social networks of parents and their children.* New York: Cambridge University Press.

Coles, R. (1989). *The call of stories.* Boston: Houghton Mifflin.

Corno, L. (1989). What it means to be literate about classrooms. In David Bloom (Ed.), *Classrooms and literacy* (pp. 29–52). Norwood, NJ: Ablex Publishing Corp.

Davies, D. (1988 as cited in White-Clark & Becker, 1996). The "hard-to-reach" parent. *Old challenges, new insights.* Fairfax, VA: National Community Education Association.

Edwards, P. A. (1990). *Parents as partners in reading: A family literacy training program.* Chicago: Children's Press.

Edwards, P. A. (1993). *Parents as partners in reading: A family literacy training program.* Second Edition. Chicago: Children's Press.

Edwards, P. A. (1995). Combining parents' and teachers' thoughts about storybook reading at home and school. In L. M. Morrow (Ed.), *Family literacy: Multiple perspectives to enhance literacy development* (pp. 54–60). Newark, DE: International Reading Association.

Edwards, P. A. (2004). *Children's literacy development: Making it happen through school, family, and community involvement.* Boston: Allyn & Bacon.

Edwards, P. A. (2007). Home literacy environments: What we know and need to know. In M. Pressley, A. Bilman, K. Perry, K. Refitt, & J. Reynolds (Eds.), *Shaping literacy achievement: Research we have, research we need* (pp. 42–76). New York: Guilford Press.

Edwards, P. A., Pleasants, H. M., & Franklin, S. H. (1999). *A path to follow: Learning to listen to parents.* Portsmouth, NH: Heinemann.

Epstein, J. L. (1988). How do we improve programs for parent involvement? *Educational Horizons, 66*(2), 58–59.

Epstein, J. L. (2001). *School, family, and community partnerships: Preparing educators and improving schools.* Boulder, CO: Westview.

Garner, B. (1991). *Improving student grades in middle school mathematics through a homework policy involving automated daily parent contact.* Fort Lauderdale, FL: Nova Southeastern University. (ERIC Document No. ED 350 142.)

Glazer, N. T., & Williams, S. (2001). Averting the homework crisis. *Educational Leadership, 58*(7) 43–45.

Hartman, C. (2002). High classroom turnover: How children get left behind. In D. M. Piche, W. L. Taylor, & R. A. Reed (Eds.), *Rights at risk: Equality in an age of terrorism* (pp. 227–244). Washington, DC: Citizens Commission on Civil Rights.

Harwayne, S. (1999). *Going public: Priorities & practices at the Manhattan New School.* Portsmouth, NH: Heinemann.

Henderson, A., Marburger, C. L., & Ooms, T. (1986). *Beyond the bake sale: An educator's guide to working with parents.* Columbia, MD: National Committee for Citizens in Education.

Kerbow, D. (1996). *Patterns of urban student mobility and local school reform.* (ERIC Document No. ED 402 386.)

Kohn, A. (2006a). *The homework myth: Why our kids get too much of a bad thing.* Cambridge, MA: Da Capo Press.

Kohn, A. (2006b). Abusing research: The study of homework and other examples. *Phi Delta Kappan, 88*(1), 9–22.

Kralovec, E., & Buell, J. (2000). *The end of homework: How homework disrupts families, overburdens children, and limits learning.* Boston: Beacon.

Li, G. (2006). *Culturally contested pedagogy: Battles of literacy and schooling between mainstream teachers and Asian immigrant parents.* Albany, NY: SUNY Press.

Manning, M., Morrison,G., & Camp, D. (2009). *Creating the best literacy book ever: A framework for successfully managing, teaching, and assessing in an extended literacy block.* New York: Scholastic.

Marzano, R. J., & Pickering, D. J. (2007). Special topic/The case for and against homework. *Educational Leadership, 64*(6), 74–79.

Maslow, A. (1943). A theory of human motivation, *Psychological Review*, vol. 50, 1943, 370–96.

McGill-Franzen, A., & Allington, R. L. (1991). Every child's right: Literacy. *The Reading Teacher, 45,* 86–90.

No Child Left Behind Act of 2001. Pub. L. No. 107–110, 115 Stat, 1425 (2002).

Popp, P. A. (2004). *Reading on the go! Students who are highly mobile and reading instruction.* Prepared for the National Center for Homeless Education. Washington, DC: U. S. Department of Education.

Popp, P. A., Stronge, J. H., & Hindman, J. L. (2003). *Students on the move: Reaching and teaching highly mobile children and youth.* National Center for Homeless Education at SERVE & ERIC Clearinghouse on Urban Education.

Purkey, W. W., & Novak, J. M. (1984). *Inviting school success: A self-concept approach to teaching and learning.* Belmont, CA: Wadsworth.

Sang, H. A. (1986). T.V., telephones, and teachers bring homework help to kids. *The Executive Educator, 8,* 25–26.

Seefeldt, C. (1985). Communicate with curriculum. *Day Care and Early Education, 13*(2), 22–25.

Swap, S. M. (1987). *Enhancing parent involvement in schools: A manual for parents and teachers.* New York: Teachers College Press.

Taylor, D., & Dorsey-Gaines, C. (1988). *Growing up literate: Learning from inner-city families.* Portsmouth, NH: Heinemann.

Vandergrift, J. A., & Greene, A. L. (1992). Rethinking parent involvement. *Educational Leadership, 50* (1), 57–59.

White-Clark, R., & Decker, L. E. (1996). *The "hard-to-reach" parent: Old challenges, new insights.* Fairfax, VA: National Community Education Association.

Winters, W. G. (1993). *African American mothers and urban schools: The power of participation.* New York: Lexington Books.

About the Author

Patricia A. Edwards is a Distinguished Professor of Teacher Education and a Senior University Outreach Fellow at Michigan State University. She is also the recipient of the prestigious Michigan State University 1994 Teacher-Scholar Award and the 2001 Distinguished Faculty Award. She holds a Bachelor of Science Degree in Elementary Education from Albany State University (Albany, GA); a Master of Science Degree in Elementary Education from North Carolina A & T University (Greensboro, NC); an Educational Specialist Degree in Reading Education from Duke University (Durham, NC); and a Doctor of Philosophy Degree in Reading Education from the University of Wisconsin–Madison (Madison, WI).

She was a member of the Board of Directors of the International Reading Association from May 1998 to May 2001 and served from December 2006 to December 2007 as the first African-American President of the National Reading Conference (NRC). NRC is the world's premier reading research organization. Edwards has served as an advisor to the First National Goal "Readiness for School," and the Michigan State University Institute for Families, Youth, and Children. She is the newly elected Vice-President of the International Reading Association (IRA). She will serve as Vice President of the Association in 2008–2009, as President-Elect in 2009–2010, and as President in 2010–2011.

She is a nationally recognized expert in parent involvement, home, school, community partnerships, multicultural literacy, early literacy, and family/intergenerational literacy, especially among poor and minority families. She is the author of *A Path to Follow: Learning to Listen to Parents* (Heinemann, 1999) and *Children's Literacy Development: Making It Happen Through School, Family, and Community Involvement* (Allyn & Bacon, 2004), as well as three forthcoming books, *It's Time for Straight Talk: When White Teachers Teach in Multicultural Settings* (Heinemann), *The Sankofa Spirit of Literacy: Looking Back to Move Forward in Educating African American Students* (Teachers College Press), and *Best Practices in ELL Instruction* (Guilford Press).